ALMOST
The Road to the Grande

By
Tom McAuliffe

NEXT STOP PARADISE PUBLISHING
Ft. Walton Beach, Florida, USA

ALMOST
The Road to the Grande

by Tom McAuliffe

Copyright © 2023 - All rights reserved.

Any references to historical events, real people, or real places are factual to the best of the authors memory, research and public records.

All rights to their respective holders. Educational-Historical documentation this non-profit publication is permitted by Fair Use copyright law.

First Edition - 2023
Second Edition - 2024

PRINT ISBN # 979-8-9892712-3-8
eBook ISBN # 979-8-9892712-4-5
Audiobook ISBN # 979-8-9892712-5-2

Please Leave us a Review!

For more information email:
bookinfo@nextstopparadise.com

WWW.AUTHORTOMMCAULIFFE.COM

DEDICATIONS

To all the bands and musicians that poured their sweat and hearts into their shows at the local dance and eventually at the Grande.

To Russ Gibb for making it all possible.

For my wife Sharon the original rocker!

Of Note:
This is a non-profit Fair Use book and <u>all the profits are being donated in the name of Grande Founder Russ Gibb</u>; 50% to the American Heart Association (he died of a heart attack) and 50% to the National Association for the Reform of Marijuana Laws (NORMAL).

This book is to honor the forgotten, the overlooked heroes and foot-soldiers of the glory days of Michigan music from 1965 to 1975 a magic decade. It is sadly incomplete and requires much more input from those who were there... those who cheered, those who hitched, those who copped fake ID's, those who made Boone's Farm an institution. It is also for those who humped heavy equipment across parking lots and up stairs in the heat, the cold and the rain...and those who stayed out pass parental curfew! This book will be revised in 2024 with a 2nd Edition... so PLEASE get your recollections and photos in to us to make it REALLY complete. WE THANK YOU!

LONG LIVE MICHIGAN ROCK-N-ROLL!

TABLE OF CONTENTS

PREFACE 9

FORWARD 17

Chapter 1 The Detroit Scene 23

Chapter 2 The Bands! 31

Chapter 3 The Communiqués 87

Chapter 4 The Clubs 91

Chapter 5 Records Go Round & Round 99

Chapter 6 The Ann Arbor Connection 103

Chapter 7 Power to the People 113

Chapter 8 Detroit Radio 119

Chapter 9 Here, There and Everywhere 125

Chapter 10 The Influencers 139

Chapter 11 The Boy Howdy Story 149

Chapter 12 Pictures & Clips 153

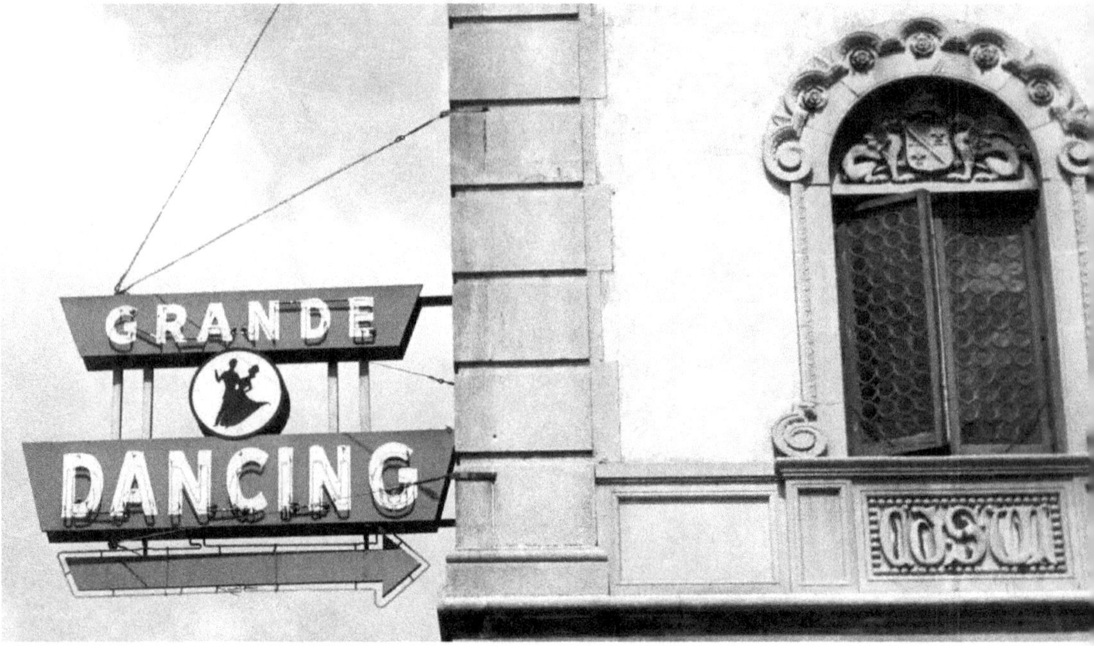
GRANDE
DANCING

DETROIT

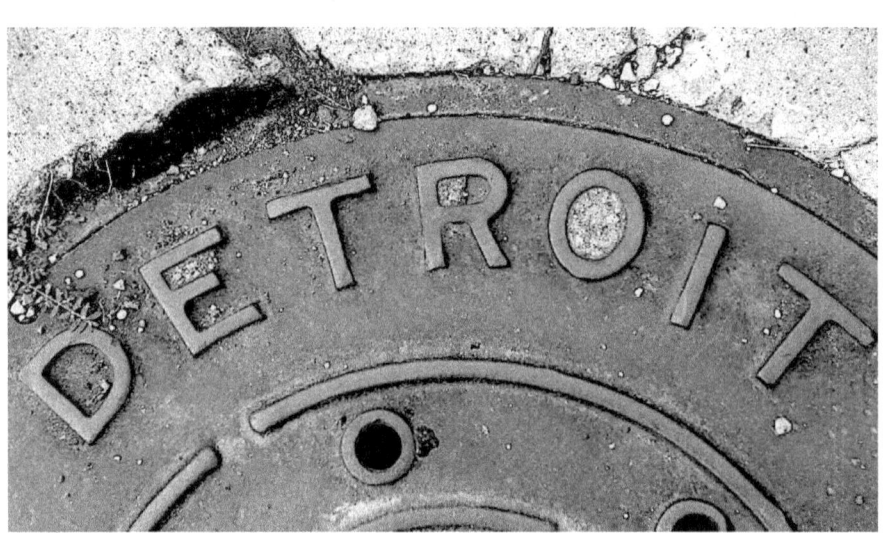

PREFACE

It was hot and humid like a southern night in August with no AC. The smoky air covered me like a wet blanket. The Bassline started and built like a freight train leaving the station. The Drums joined in and began thumping my chest as a Guitar cut in with a Psychedelic 12 bar blues and the vocals began a chant. It was a band I had never heard of, 'The Frost' from of all places Alpena, Michigan on the right side of the mitten deep in the great white north. Not exactly a hotbed of show business. The tune, 'Rock-n-Roll Music', had 'Hit' written all over it and was better than 90% of the hits on the radio in 1968. It became an anthem.

The Grande Ballroom on Grand River Avenue in Detroit was a historic music venue known for hosting rock concerts during the late 1960s and early 1970s. It had a capacity of only approximately 1,500 people which made it an intimate place to see a concert. There were no seats and there was no AC and in the winter heat was minimal.

The world class dance hall was built in 1928 by architect Charles Agree and had acoustics that rivaled any venue anywhere. From Big bands in the 1930s and 40s to Do Whop in the 1950s to the popular acts of 1960s it was the place to be for music and dancing. Beginning in 1966 when a local high school teacher created it until its semi-closure The Grande became the cross roads of Rock-n-Roll for both US as well as UK bands.

Teacher Russ Gibb's palace had a stage that saw acts like Cream, The Who, Rod Stewart, CCR, The Byrds, Three Dog Night and it had an old fashioned hardwood dance floor, the largest in America at the time, to boogie the night away on. When my Mom could not find me it was because I had taken the bus to The Grande.

But these national and international bands were not the only 'stars' to take the stage there. The Detroit and Ann Arbor communities had their very own stars like SRC, Savage Grace, The Rationals, UP, 3rd Power, The Gang, Frijid Pink and The Frost… to name just a few. To us they were, and in some cases still are, local rock gods! However for whatever reason; luck, money, drugs, politics or musical differences, these bands never saw national exposure and success nor sometimes even local recognition. This book hopes to examine and address that… at least a little bit.

With first hand accounts from the musicians and patrons of our beloved venues, 'Almost' documents these awesome lesser known acts; what they did then and what they are doing now. It is high time these standing ovation worthy bands are acknowledged and documented for history. This book hopes to help address this lack of recognition and document these world class musicians and this special time in musical history. We will try to cover new information that other efforts haven't and this will be an ongoing project as we get info on these bands.

Springing forth from the Detroit high school and Teen Dance Club scene thee rock concert venue was 'The

Grande' and many a local band saw playing there as the pinnacle of rock-n-roll success... at least in Michigan. I love these bands and this is their story.

In the summer of 2023 on one of the many Facebook pages dedicated to Detroit music I met lots of fellow fans there including some CREEM Magazine alums. To show what a small world it is... I did an Internship there during my senior year at Seaholm High School in Birmingham Michigan. After moving from Walled Lake the CREEM offices were just around the corner from The Palladium concert hall. I conversing we bemoaned the fact that most of the bands we grew up with and came to know and love never got their due props. We're doin something about it.

In my teenage Detroit days I had the feeling of being in the eye of an invisible storm... a person standing on the platform around the fastest Waltzer ever.... watching a kaleidoscope, lost in space, time and perception... nothing stuck in my memory except for the sense of the maelstrom. Every band I saw seemed better than the last and they were, for the most part, very polished. And I was there or I was out playing a gig with my band.

Publications like The Fifth Estate, the Detroit News and CREEM Magazine all gave some oxygen to the clubs, high schools and Teen-fests... and also to the bands that played the circuit. And, since these media reached across the entire Detroit/Ann Arbor metroplex... the kids became connected. They went to the shows, heard the bands and read the articles... and the entire 'scene' grew exponentially... like compound interest. And soon, other opportunities rose and young fans had different ways to experience their music both live and in print. They were hungry.

For example one of Detroit's major retail stores Hudsons opened up a brand new mall in Oakland in July '69 and, to promote it, they decided to throw a "Drive-in" concert, featuring Bob Seger playing to 20,000 kids - his biggest crowd ever up to that point, also on the bill was 'Savage Grace' and 'Sky', two very popular local bands.

At one point, when Hudson's was still a downtown store, they even had some small lunchtime rock shows inside the store. Several local bands played these peculiar concerts but they were very successful and drew decent crowds from the same kinda lunchtime crowds that used to sneak away to the Cavern to see the Beatles.

At the time a group of alleged 'Movers and Shakers'… including media, managers, booking agents, equipment renters and the sixties version of social media-which was mostly girls who 'got around' a lot, got together! It was a whole new social/musical/theatrical order and even the retail world that stretched from the Hudsons giant middle-America department stores to the quaint Haight-inspired Plum Street "hippie" Head Shop emporiums with the incense, candles, kaftan and beads, took part. Whenever someone came up with an idea.. no matter how unique and seemingly impossible… no-one suggested that it couldn't be done… they just did it. Sometimes it worked and sometimes it failed. And it was

into this whirligig of action, music, media and excitement that one flourished – against all odds.

One was hypnotized by the waltzers and transfixed by the music. My ever-expanding ego made me arrogant and selfish, conceited and irresponsible. I was rubbing elbows with the leaders of the local rock community.

In '68-69… you could see three bands a day… all quite different, almost all with their own original compositions. For the most part these bands were young and inexperienced to be sure but they were alive with feverish creative musical excitement and they were willing to work thirty hours a day to get better. You could feel their commitment and sense their complete joy at actually being in a rock-n-roll band. They contained some of the best musicians, singers and writers that I have ever heard–even today.

Born and bred in Detroit, McAuliffe was there and for this book he interviewed those who lived it; Musicians, Agents, Bookers, Fans and Roadies…. these are their tales of teen clubs, high school dances and music festivals playing the sounds of rock-n-roll around Michigan and of course at The Grande and other venues like it. He has always felt local Detroit Bands have never gotten the respect nor credit they deserve and the time

from 1965-1972 was the golden years where Detroit was the headquarters of rock and these Michigan bands influenced music worldwide.

And that's what this book is about… the NFL has college players to pick from, Baseball has farm teams to find talent… the Detroit and Michigan music scenes had The

Grande, and the other clubs, all with a huge pool of talent, born and honed in the network of clubs, dances, festivals and free concert gigs in various parks... It all led to one place but it was the scene that made them the awesome bands they eventually became... This is the well told story of their journeys!

The many folks who have helped to create this book and I, have tried to be as accurate as possible while not getting in the way of the story. It was more than 55 years ago but it feels like yesterday and as I look back at my life it was moments created by these local musicians that stand out and are still vivid in my mind. To them I say THANK YOU and I hope you enjoy it!

Tom

Of Note: *If you were in one of these bands please get in touch as we plan on regular updates with new Editions and would like to include you! In the meantime please scope us out at our Facebook Page:*
FB.com/AlmostroadtotheGrande.com

FORWARD

Lovin, Loud and Proud
Credit Where Credit is Due

By Tony D'Anninzio

This book is to honor the forgotten, the overlooked, the heroes and foot soldiers of the glory days of Michigan Rock-n-Roll music during the 1960s. It was a magic time where the local bands performed on the same stage as the International heavyweights. But this book, which is also helping to raise money for charity in Uncle Russ's name, is also for those who hustled heavy equipment across parking lots and up stairs in the heat, the snow and the rain. And it's also for all those who have memories of staying out past parental curfew to hear the music.

Do you remember? Can you still hear the music? Here we focus on the bands and venues from 1965 to 1972 - the ones which had not been recognized by the music world at the time and which still tend to get ignored in the general history of Michigan Rock'n'Roll. Not just bands and clubs from Detroit and the burbs... but the entire state. Gigs from school dances and teen clubs that kept alive and encouraged the up and coming bands of Michigan leading up to their appearance at the big venue... The Grande Ballroom.

From its opening in 1966 till it closed only 7 years later more than 250 bands, both local and from around the world, played there. Since I created the Emmy awarding winning film 'Louder Than Love' as I travel there's not a day that goes by where someone doesn't come up to me with a great Grande Ballroom story. The music made there and the hall itself are ingrained memories for anyone who passed thru the doors at Beverly and Grand River Avenue and even for many who didn't.

The acoustics of the world-famous concert hall, which was constructed in 1928 by architect Charles Agree and rivaled those of any venue any where. It was thee place to go for music and dancing during the 1930s, 1940s, 1950s, and 1960s, from big bands in the 1930s and 1940s to do-whop in the 1950s to popular rock performers in the 1960s. Beginning in 1966, a local high school teacher and personal friend, was responsible for transforming The Grande Ballroom into a crossroads of rock-n-roll bands from the USA and England. Teacher Russ Gibb's palace had an old-fashioned hardwood dance floor, at one time the largest in America, and a stage that hosted performances by popular artists such as Cream, The Who, Rod Stewart, Led Zepplin, BB King, CCR, and Three Dog Night to name but a few.

Here McAuliffe also explores the impact that CREEM Magazine, the 5th Estate underground newspaper and even the daily Detroit News had on creating the unique alternative community that became Detroit and Ann Arbor in the late 1960's. These publications were a beacon to the disenfranchised and launched and

nourished the careers and attitudes of a generation of writers (including Tom), artists, photographers and even musicians. These publications would fire the musical dreams of the teenagers abandoned throughout the nation, terrifying their parents and teachers and becoming the most iconoclastic publications of the era...Boy Howdy indeed!

The impact the Michigan bands that played the Grande was felt long after it officially closed. And that is especially true of the many local bands who played their hearts out and were having influence on the bands from the UK. These bands came over to play the Grande as

their first foray into America. Many absorbed some Motown licks to take back to Europe with them. The additionally cross-influence of the Motown label and its artists also helped to shine a international light on the rock bands playing the Grande and other concert halls in Detroit and across the state. From the Rationals and SRC to Savage Grace, Bob Seger and the MC5 as well as lesser know local bands like The Gang, The Bossmen and The Bouys… one could hear that these groups were on par with anything coming from across the pond. So I'm proud to help shine a light on these lesser known bands and musicians and help give them the credit they so richly deserve. As a Detroit native, award winning author Tom McAuliffe has done a wonderful job in helping to document these bands and the venues that allowed fans to experience their global talents.

To say that Detroit was the epicenter of 60s rock-n-roll one only need look at the many UK bands, now household names, that were first seen in America by appearing several times at the Grande. Anyone who was actively involved with the Michigan music scene in the late 60's and early 70s will read real relevance in these pages. These local bands and their contributions to the sound of Michigan Rock-n-Roll music must not be forgotten. 'Almost-The Road to the Grande' is not a rehash of events just thrown together to milk the name for a few more dollars, besides it's for charity so it's not about money. This book is for anyone who knows and loves these relatively unknown bands or wishes they did. I think Uncle Russ is smiling down upon us now. Enjoy!

Tony D'Anninzio is the Emmy award winning Producer and Director of the film 'Louder Than Love – the Grande Ballroom Story" shown on PBS and available on Amazon. Please visit www.thegrandeballroomstory.com

CHAPTER 1

The Detroit Scene
Woodward to Grand River and Back - Oh My!

"A gig at the Grande was like... WOW! Tell everybody."
Guitarist Mark Farner, Grand Funk Rail Road

It was the 1960s in one of, at the time, the most exciting cities on the planet. We made cars—the four-wheeled dream machines that America rode on. Detroit, after the Second World War, was the place to be. Growth and innovation were its middle names. Add to the industrial mix a rich blues and jazz history, and it was a wonderful place to live and grow up. The city is laid out with a central downtown where Cobo Hall and the Olympia were located, and then three major roads leading out to the suburbs: Gratiot Ave. to the east, Woodward Ave. up the middle, and Grand River Ave. to the west. The bus system made it easy for folks to get from the suburbs to downtown, quickly and inexpensively.

Detroit was a vibrant and dynamic city... still is. It had a booming automotive industry, with companies like Ford, General Motors, and Chrysler playing a significant role in the city's economy. This led to an influx of jobs and a prosperous middle class, with many residents working in the automotive factories.

However, the 1960s also saw the city grappling with significant social and economic challenges. Racial tensions were high, and Detroit experienced several race-related riots, including the disastrous 1967 Detroit Riots. These events highlighted deep-seated racial inequality and systemic issues within the city.

Additionally, the city's population started to decline in the late 1960s due to factors such as suburbanization and deindustrialization. Some say the city died in the riots of '67, the results of which led to the continuing deterioration of some neighborhoods and an increase in crime. The flight to the suburbs had begun!

Despite the challenges of the city, Detroit still had a vibrant cultural scene. In 1959 Motown Records was founded by Berry Gordy Jr., achieved tremendous success during this time, introducing the world to 'The Sound of Young America' and influential music artists that helped break down racial barriers. Motown's unique blend of soul, R&B, and pop music had a profound

impact on American music overall, and Detroit was again ground zero. I can remember taking the bus down Grand River and going to the Fox Theater to see The Motown Revu with Stevie Wonder, The Temptations, Four Top, Supreams, and more. But that's another story for another time. Suffice it to say that anyone growing up in Detroit, was in a rich cultural playground be it rock or soul music.

Every vocation needs a place to learn, gain experience, grow as an artist, and gain some chops. Such is true for musicians. When Bob Dylan plugged in at the New Port Jazz Festival in 1964 popular music went electric, and the youth of America would never be the same. Rock-n-Roll bands in Michigan and the Detroit area during the early 1960s were fortunate that there were so many avenues to share their talents and music. Parties, special events, and high school dances were happening across the state usually employing a local band. In Detroit, Catholic Central High School, Christ the King, and St. Mary's… all had dances (called 'Sock Hops' because you would take off your shoes). Additionally the Catholic

Church booked a lot of bands at the time. Add to that the public schools like Gross Pointe High, Redford High School, Seaholm Hugh School, and many others, they all had dances once, sometimes even twice a month. Anything to keep kids off the streets was the mentality of those in charge. And that was fine with us. Like the song says, "It's 'got to be rock and roll music if you want to dance with me!" And we did.

In the 1960s, Detroit experienced a vibrant counterculture movement, and head shops played a significant role in this scene. Head Shops were stores that catered to the young hippie and the bohemian subculture, offering various items related to counterculture, spirituality, and self-expression. They became popular gathering spots for like-minded individuals seeking an alternative lifestyle and a place to find unique products. These shops were known for their wide range of merchandise, including psychedelic posters, tie-dye clothing, rolling papers, incense, smoking accessories, and various paraphernalia associated with the use of mind-altering substances. They were often decorated with colorful and eclectic displays, giving off an inviting and psychedelic atmosphere. Aside from selling products, head shops also served as cultural hubs, acting as meeting places for artists, musicians, and activists. Music played a crucial role in these establishments, with popular tunes from rock, folk, and psychedelic genres often playing in the background. While head shops were undoubtedly popular during this time, it's worth noting that the counterculture movement faced both support and backlash, with some establishments facing legal challenges due to the sale of drug paraphernalia. However, they remained an integral part of the city's cultural landscape, embodying the spirit of rebellion, self-expression, and social change that defined the 60s.

In addition to the public and parochial schools that booked thousands of bands over the decade, there were also tons of 'Teen Cubs' where alcohol was not served but large doses of rock music were: The Hideout, Bookies, The Chessmate, 20 Grand, Westside 6, Village Pub, Something Different, The Kit Kat Club, The Top Hat, and lots more. While no exact count exists, folks who were that indicate that in SE Michigan alone there were more than 100 Teen Clubs (clubs that catered to the teen market and did not serve alcohol.) Add to that dances at the VFW's, American Legion's, Elks Clubs, and Moose lodges that also booked local talent on a regular basis and one can see it was a fertile gig market and musical training ground. All these venues allowed three-chord musicians to hone their talent with the dancing youth of Michigan. The teen clubs and school dances paved the way for the larger, more swanky clubs and concert venues that were to come. Later, I indulged my musical passions in places like The Eastown, The Vanity, and the Carrousel Ballroom. (I was there the night The J. Giles Band recorded what I think is one of the best live rock-n-roll records ever created. 'Full House'.)

The great need for the local alternative/hippie/freak community to have local venues for music and camaraderie was also fulfilled. It provided a fun way for youth to dance the night, and in some cases, an afternoon

away. It's one thing to be playing 3-4 chord rock in the garage or basement, but it is quite another to be playing music before a live audience. And hearing a record is not the same as a live band. Some musicians are fine playing in a basement, but put them on stage with a live audience of dancing youth, and they freeze like deer in headlights.

Later in the mid-to late-60s, more concert venues opened, such as The Eastown, The Palladium, The Carousel Ballroom, The Vanity Ballroom, and, of course, the dance hall that was the start of it all, The Grande Ballroom. Many of these were converted movie palaces from the 30s and 40s and featured great acoustics and ornate art deco-like designs. These venues not only allowed local bands to tune up their performances, but they also provided major bands from the UK to easily cut their teeth in America to enthusiastic crowd responses. Foremost among these concert halls was The Downtown's answer to the more famous Bill Graham's Fillmore East in the East Village area of New York City and the Fillmore west located in San Francisco. Built in 1926 and fully open in 1928, The Grande hosted Big Band music for years and featured the largest hardwood dance floor in America at the time. An interesting note is

that the dance all on Boblo island became #1 as it also had a wooden floor and could hold 5000 dancers at once.

Music and the new 'Woodstock' culture came quickly, and almost overnight there were head shops with posters, beads, and incense and rock-n-roll record stores in almost every neighborhood. Of course, there were many in the community who fought having these shops and dances by by kids dancing to the 'evil devil of rock-n-roll', but they were for the most part unsuccessful. I can remember when my Dad made my sisters take down their Beatles posters in their bedroom, and when the boys from Liverpool hit the Ed Sullivan TV show, the entire family let him know it was going to be watched. Dad left and went to the 'Beer Garden.' We watched on a 19' Zenith black-and-white TV, and while my mom rolled her eyes and my sisters swooned, I stared at the screen in astonishment. It was a fundamental cultural shift that I have only now come to fully appreciate. It was like when JFK got shot or the Tiger won the series. You remember when there was a before and an after dividing line. The ground-breaking shift was under way, and soon even straight middle-class automobile executives were in bell bottoms with long side burns and paisley prints.

After the riots of 1967, the city needed some good news and got it with baseball. The '68 Detroit Tigers were a baseball wonder, winning the World Series. Black or white, young or old, everyone loved the Tigers, and it offered a unique opportunity for young and old fans alike to communicate and re-bond. By 1968, the Vietnam War was also raging, and the college campuses in Lansing, Ann Arbor, and Detroit had what seemed like constant protests with sit-ins at all the schools and universities.

I have vivid recollections of one anti-war parade in 1969... we marched up Woodward Ave. and then encircled the Armed Forces Induction Center. Then all the protesters held hands and tried to levitate the building off the ground! These events of civil disobedience provided an opportunity for those who hated the war and loved rock-n-roll to bond and share notes.

All in all, the 1960s were an exciting time for rock music in Detroit and across America. The city birthed numerous rock and soul bands and artists that left a lasting impact on music. Their music continues to inspire and resonate with fans all around the world.

CHAPTER 2

The Bands, the Bands, the Bands!
3 chords never sounded so good

"If it's illegal to rock and roll, throw my ass in jail!"
Kurt Cobain

Your favorite band may be one that nobody has ever heard of, but to you, they are the second coming. The mid-60's to early 1970s were a golden time in Rock-n-Roll, and Detroit and the Grande were at the center of all of it. Springing from the teen club and school dance circuit of the early to mid-60's, these bands honed their chops and usually set a two-fold goal: play the Grande or Cobo and get a record deal. Some made it but many did not. Having a circuit of regular school dances and teen clubs was crucial to these bands honing their craft and developing their musical chops (their playing prowess) and stage performance skills so that they could graduate to larger venues like The Grande, Cobo Hall, festivals, and out-of-state gigs.

As rock became more popular, the instruments of the folk age faded away, or at least into the background. The mid-60s saw the explosion of electric guitar-based bands. Popular instruments of the day include, as now, Fender and Gibson guitars, Ludwig or Rogers drums, Sunn, Vox, and Fender amps. Shure Vocalmaster PA's and Padded Kustom red or orange amps were in use, but many garage bands used PA amplifiers made by companies such as Fender, Gibson, and Ampeg and plugged all the guitars and mics into them. These amplifiers were popular for their cost, reliability, and versatility, and they could handle the high volume and distortion that were typical of rock music. These portable PA systems could be easily transported to gigs and rehearsals. And perhaps amazingly, to today's artists, they never used an auto-tune device for vocals. Instead, they sang on key.

Local bands had a mid-1960s set list that changed a lot with the British Invasion. Some iconic songs from this era that bands had on their Set Lists included:

The Kingsmen: Louie Louie

The Beatles: A Hard Day's Night, I Wanna Hold Your Hand, Drive My Car

The Rolling Stones: Satisfaction, Paint It Black, and Get Off My Cloud

The Beach Boys: Good Vibrations, Surfin' USA, California Girls

The Doors: Light My Fire, Break on Through, People Are Strange

The Who: My Generation, Pinball Wizard, I Can't Explain

The Kinks: You Really Got Me, Waterloo Sunset, Lola

The Byrds: Turn! Turn! Turn! Mr. Tambourine Man, Eight Miles High

These are just a few examples, but there were countless other songs that young people were dancing to, not just in the big D but everywhere in Michigan.

The Detroit's scene soon grew and spilled over across the entire state. Notable Michigan bands from other parts of the state like Flint, Apena, and Traverse City, started to make inroads and get more gigs (jobs) in the big city. A few of the popular bands from that era who were not based in or from Detroit include: The Frost, originally from Alpena, The MC5 from Lincoln Park, The Rationals from Ann Arbor...and tons more.

These are just a few examples of Michigan bands from the 1960s that were *not* from or based in Detroit. There were undoubtedly many other talented groups throughout the state during that time, each contributing to the rich musical landscape of the great lake state.

The bands of the time influenced culture and their fans and through the music they helped bring about the end of the Vietnam War. Sadly, while these bands were local stars, they were never really recognized outside of the Motor City. They affected rock music worldwide but never got the fame, money or recognition they deserved. Their music was every bit as polished and professional as the bands coming over from the UK and it was clear the two were influencing each other. Bands from Motown had great rhythm sections while UK bands always had great vocal harmonies and the two intertwined.

The reader will notice that the MC5, Iggy etc. are not really mentioned here. This is because they have already been written about… a lot. If your band is not included, please get in touch, as we will be doing a second edition in 2024 and would like to have your band onboard. This book is about the more unknown groups we don't know but should, and these are their brief bios! We plan on doing an Edition every year so please get in touch. These bands deserve to be documented for history!

BAND BIOs

S R C (The Scott Richard Case)
Formerly The Fugitives and The Ravins
SRC, short for Scott Richard Case, was indeed a rock band from Detroit in the 1960s. The group was formed in 1966 and gained popularity for their psychedelic and hard rock sound. SRC's music blended elements of blues, rock, and psychedelia, similar to other bands of the era. SRC released a few albums throughout their career,

including their self-titled debut album 'SRC' in 1968, which featured the popular track 'Black Sheep'. The band's lineup went through some changes over the years, but they continued to be active until 1972.

Their initial gigs were varied; Cobo Hall Teen Fair, a Frat Party at U of M Campus, a Teen Sock Hop at Fitzgerald High School in Warren, MI, for CKLW radio, and playing at Mother's Teenage Nightclub up north in East Tawas, Michigan, were some of the band's first gigs, but later concerts at The Palladium in Birmingham, The Vanity and Grande Ballrooms, and one of SRC's largest gigs was opening for the Ike & Tina Turner Review at the U of M's huge Hill Auditorium.

While SRC didn't achieve huge commercial success, they were highly regarded in the Motor City music scene at the time. Their sound was known for its heavy guitar riffs and energetic performances. Since then, fans of classic rock and the psychedelic sub-genre have grown to appreciate SRC's music.

Guitar players Gary Quackenbush and Steve Lyman got together in the mid-60s to form what became one of the premier Detroit rock-n-roll bands of the late 1960s and early 1970s. However, before SRC became quintessential, they went through a few name changes: first The Fugitives, then The Ravins, then Scot Richard Case, and eventually SRC for short and they soon joined Ann Arbor talent booker Hugh "Jeep" Holland's A2 Talent Agency and planned on a album on his label.

The mid-70s saw SRC still trying to get some national traction, renaming themselves 'Blue Scepter'... They were dropped by CBS Records in 1971, and that was the end of the road. But of all the bands we surveyed here, SRC drew the most responses.

"I remember seeing SRC at one of the auto shows at Cobo Hall back in, I believe, 1969. It was like a custom/classic car show vis-à-vis the big international one. I remember they blew me away with their cover of Heatwave. I wish I could be more exact about the date, but I'm pretty sure, based on the girl I took, that it was 1969! I also remember the Buddy Miles-SRC show at the Palladium in Birmingham; it was fantastic."
-Tom

"I have been a fan of SRC since the late 1960s. I have their first album on vinyl, as well as a few MP3's from other albums. I keep trying to get more. They were an excellent band, and nothing will ever replace psychedelic rock. It's still my favorite type of music."
-George

"I saw SRC in Jackson at the 'Armory.' It seems like it was May of 1970 on a Friday night. I was 15 and owned the first album. It was a great show with a lot of songs from Traveler's Tale. I had strict parents and never got to the Grande, but I followed via WKNR a lot of Michigan bands."
-Jerry

Ushering in a more psychedelic sound, Detroit's SRC is one band that should've received a wider audience and

more success on the radio and in record sales.
LINE UP
Gary J. Quackenbush - Guitar / Vocals - RIP
Steve Lyman - Guitairst
Glenn Quackenbush - Organ
Steve Lyman - Rhythm guitar / Vocals
Robin Dale / Al Wilmot - Bass / Vocals
E. G. Clawson / Scott Williamson - Drums

Patterns

Another popular but relatively unknown band is Patterns. Playing high-energy covers and originals to the Michigan masses, they touched thousands. They were high school friends getting together to make some good music and get the people dancing! The band played everywhere, from dances at Carrini and Allen Park High Schools to concerts at the Caraway Ballroom and eventually the Grande. Concert goers took notice.

"Some of our members were in bands before, like Springwell, Rogues, Intrigues, and Underground Wall. They played at the Grande with the Underground Wall, opened for Albert King, and were regulars at the Grande during its heyday. Seeing Springwell and The Rumor play local gigs was awesome," said Guitarist Russ Tkac. "Filling in for Mark Ballentine on bass for the band 'Springwell' in 1974 for a concert with 300-500 people outdoors in London, Ontario, was a gas! The mid to late 1960s were such great time for both local musicians and for the people who went to see them," said Tkac. "We had a lot of local talent, and it was a very vibrant music scene with lots of gigs and things going on. But New

York and LA were the places to be and get noticed." Many local musicians had to move to try and make it.

"I didn't really have a full appreciation of the influence Detroit bands were having on the UK bands that came over to play. Others had an idea, but I was too busy creating and performing," Tkac explained. "Publications like Creem and the 5th Estate, as well as local rock stations like WABX FM, were very helpful in getting the local music and dance scenes to grow. However when the legal drinking age was lowered to 18 in 1973, it really killed the teen club scene. Most bands just played bars then," Tkac said. "It was indeed a great time for original rock music and should be remembered fondly," he said.

The band stopped actively gigging in 1974, but they still stay in touch. They now write and record music as a band called 'Bad Axe' which is a small town at the tip of the thumb in the Michigan mitten.

LINE UP
Paul Ruehl - Guitar Lead / Vocals
Russ Tkac - Lead Guitar
Kevin Milner - Guitar / Vocals
Jim Redden - Bass / Vocals
Scott Dula - Drums
Jeff Bowdell - Drums
Terry Sullivan - Lead Guitar

The Rationals

The Rationals came together in 1964 to create one of the most soulful and popular bands in Detroit 1960s rock-n-roll. The following year, they cut their debut single for

Jeep Holland's local label, known as A2 Records, out of Ann Arbor. They initially had good success with the original song 'Gave My Love' and then went on to record a cover of Otis Redding's 'Respect' which also did quite well. Because of this, they were awarded a contract with Cameo/Parkway Records for national distribution, and their single ended up reaching position #92 on the Billboard Hot 100 chart. Due to distribution difficulties, the record did not become available in all parts of the United States at the same time, making it hard to make a respectable showing on the national record charts.

But like most bands of the mid-60s The Rationals got off to a simple start. "Follow guitar player, Steve Correll and I started before everyone else. That could've been as early as '62. I was in junior high school," explained Guitaist Scott Morgan. "We were playing basic party music, which would be like instrumental tunes, which was really big at that time," he said.

The next big influence on the young player was the British invasion. "It was really fresh," said Morgan. "These guys were totally different and they wrote their own songs. People were excited by it. It started with just the Beatles, but then it moved rapidly to the Stones, the Animals, the Kinks, the Who, and then everybody else," he said. The band had a lot of influences at first. "We were listening to and trying to do covers of tunes brought to us by Jeep Holland, who became our manager right around 1964–65. He was a clerk at Discount Records in Ann Arbor, and he was also a disc jockey at the local YMCA which had weekend dances," explained Morgan.

As popular as the Rationals became locally, they could not seem to break through and achieve national success. There were some logical reasons for this, however. "Aside from all the business aspects, like moving from one label to another and never getting on one major label and staying there, to never graduating from the A2 school of running everything out of Jeep's apartment made it hard to succeed. And I think we were also just too young," said Morgan. "We didn't have very much experience and were kind of learning as we went along.

The Rationals

We didn't really know how it was done. how you get bigger, more famous, or better musically. We didn't know any of that stuff. We're just kind of making it up as we go along," Morgan said. But the bands reputation grew.

The band's subsequent singles 'I Need You' and 'Hold On Baby' were each local hits in Michigan, but again the records failed to gain traction with radio or national audiences. Even though they were the band voted 'most lightly to succeed', at least in the heads of anyone after they saw the group play. Even the author, who is a fan, thought that they were the most likely Detroit to 'make it'.

They came from humble beginnings. "Player, Steve Correll and I, started before everyone else. That could have been as early as '62. I was in eighth grade in junior high school," explained Guitarist Morgan. Vocals were not an issue. "We were playing just kind of party music, which would be like instrumental tunes, which was really big at that time." The band had a lot of influences. "We were listening to and trying to do covers of tunes brought to us by Jeep Holland, who became our manager right around 1964–'65. He was a clerk at Discount Records in Ann Arbor, and he was also a disc jockey at the local YMCA, which had weekend dances," explained Morgan. "We didn't have very much experience. We were kind of learning as we went along, and we didn't really know how it was done. How an artist gets bigger, more famous, or better performers, we didn't know any of that stuff. We were just kind of making it all up as we went along."

The Rationals did play some shows to prove they were not just another bar band. "The biggest show we ever played was Cobo Hall in 1966 when our song "Respect" was out and doing very well. We played with a bunch of other people that were really big at the time," offered Morgan. "We went onstage, and we'd never played a show this big before. It was like 10,000 screaming girls, flashbulbs going off all over and girls running up and trying to jump onto the stage and knocking over the barricades," he said. But no one was in charge, and eventually our manager just sort of walked out. He didn't even tell us he was leaving," he explained. TV and Radio personalities Robin Seymour became the de facto manager at that point. "But he didn't really know what to do with us. Eventually the band just broke up," he said.

By popular demand, The Rationals were honored by being inducted into the online Michigan Rock-n-Roll Legends Hall of Fame in 2010. Even though only being together for a short time, the band built a reputation and became known for their soulful vocals and tight

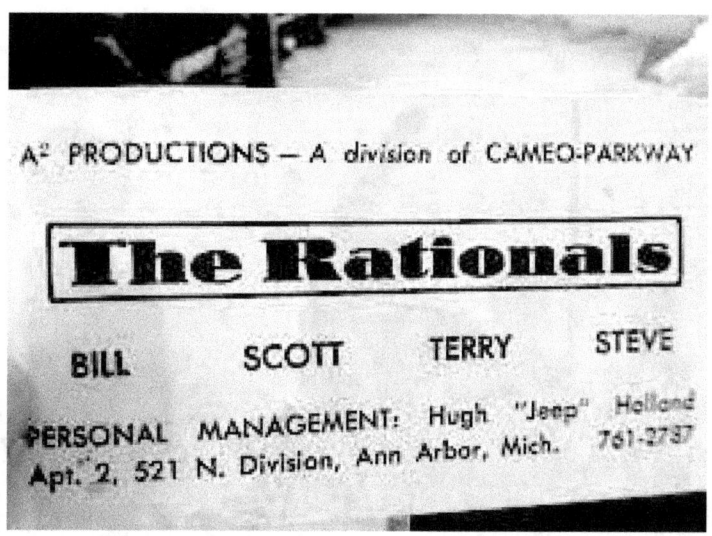

instrumentation, setting them apart from most other local bands of the time, who were looser and more like 'jam bands'. The music was and is a blend of high-energy rock and danceable soul, creating a distinctive sound.

Despite their relatively short-lived career, The Rationals left a lasting impact on the music scene and continue to be celebrated for their contributions to Michigan rock-n-roll. Morgan went on to be in the popular Sonic Rendezvous Band (SRC) with MC5 guitarist Fred Smith. He was also in the popular 1960s-70s group Guardian Angel. Morgan continues to create music today.

LINE UP
Scott Morgan – Guitar / Vocals
Steve Correll – Lead Guitar / Vocals
Bill Figg – Drums
Terry Trabandt – Bass / Vocals

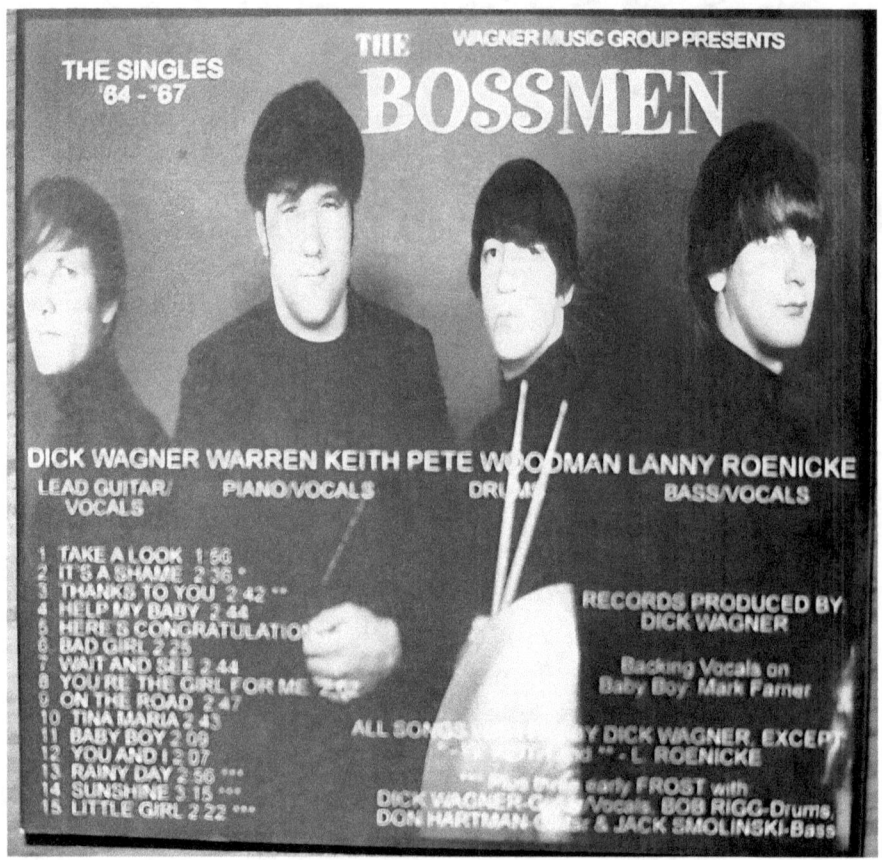

The Bossmen

The Bossmen were a band from Flint, Michigan, in the 1960s. They were formed in 1964 and gained popularity in the local area with their blend of rock and R&B music. They originally gigged a lot in Saginaw and Lansing. The band was fronted by the legendary Dick Wagner, who later became a renowned guitarist and songwriter, working with artists like Alice Cooper and Lou Reed to name but a few. Wagner became a popular and revered player in the history of Detroit Rock-n-Roll.

The Big 600 AM in Flint, WTAC, had a special event in April of 1965, and this featured Pete Woodman on drums, Lanny Roenicke on bass guitar and trumpet, and Dick 'Maestro' Wagner on guitar and vocals, with Warren Keith playing piano and vocals.

The Saginaw area band entertained central Michigan audiences. This popular quartet was initially called 'The Playboys' and was a top-40 cover band. With the addition of pianist Keith and guitarist Dick Wagner, the band evolved into The Bossmen. They released a few singles, including 'Baby Boy' and 'I Need a Love'. Their energetic live performances and catchy tunes gained them a dedicated following in mid-Michigan. While they didn't achieve national success the Bossmen were an important part of the mitten's music scene in the 1960s. Dick

Wagner's later collaborations and success in the music industry brought recognition to The Bossmen's legacy.

For a brief period, Mark Farner, later of Grand Funk Rail Road, was a member of The Bossmen. This Michigan headliner released a number of singles but Farmer was only onboard from 1964 to 1967.

LINE UP
Pete Woodman - Drums
Lanny Roenicke - Bass, Guitar & Trumpet,
Dick 'the Maestro' Wagner - Guitar / Vocals RIP
Warren Keith - Piano / Vocals

The Gang
The Gang from Detroit was formed in the early 1960s. They played at all the big time places of the day, including the Walled Lake Casino and the famed Grande. The group played everything from school dances and parties to clubs and events throughout the state. After he left the band Steve Farmer went on to enjoy national fame in The Amboy Dukes with Ted Nugent. The original Gang bass guitar player, Greg Arama, also joined Steve and Ted in the Dukes. Steve co-wrote "Journey to the Center of the Mind" with Nugent, which went to #16 on the Billboard charts in 1968.

They played the Grande early in their history and several times until the early 1970s. They then created 'The New York Touring Company', an orchestra that performed the musical play Jesus Christ Superstar, touring the USA.

Three of the founding members, Don Henderson, Jim Butler, and Steve Farmer, put the band back together in 2005 and are currently performing live in a revised version of 'The Gang' to SRO crowds.

LINE UP
Don Henderson - Lead Guitar, Keyboards, Vocals
Greg Arama -Bass
Jim Butler - Drums
Steve Farmer - Rhythm Guitar, Harmonica, Vocals
Bob Beeckman - Lead Guitar, Harmonica, Vocals
Tom Masta - Drums
Lou Fischetti - Bass / Vocals

Frijid Pink / The Detroit Vibrations

Show me a band that opened for the world-famous band Led Zeppelin and played the Grande three different times over the course of just a year, and you'll find one of the longest-gigging groups in Michigan! Starting first as 'The Detroit Vibrations' from the suburb of Allen Park and then later as the even more popular Frijid Pink, they became ground-breakers. It's thought that they were the first Detroit rock group to chart a national Top Ten single in the 1970s, 'House of the Rising Sun', and the first to have their self-titled debut LP crack the Billboard Top Twenty Albums chart. Additionally, they were one of the hardest-working bands in Michigan and spent most of their time touring on the road or in a recording studio.

Like Stevers, Harris and the other members started playing music in the school band in elementary school. Although his teacher wanted him to try the saxophone, Tom says he "wanted to play the clarinet in the woodwinds section because that's where all the girls were". His dad bought him a guitar and at the age of thirteen, he was invited to jam with his neighbor's band. They needed a bass, so they took two strings off his six-string guitar and painted it black. Harris became a bass player from that point on.

A cover band that played the current hits, The Detroit Vibrations started in 1964 in the Stevers' basement. They were basically a teen R&B band that covered Motown hits as well as the releases of many other popular artists of the day. Sadly Dan Yehley was sent to Vietnam and killed in an enemy ambush just two weeks into his deployment. The Detroit Vibrations were getting so much work that Stevers had to drop out of the high school band in his junior and senior years because he didn't have the time to participate. In late '67, the decision was made to

 play originals over a bottle of Canadian Club. As Detroit Vibrations, the band played twenty-three weekends in a row at the popular Chatterbox Club, a record. The Detroit Vibrations officially changed their name to Frijid Pink. Early shows saw the band members in pink satin outfits. Very psychedelic!

Besides ruling the stage at popular club The Chatterbox, the band regularly appeared at a variety of teen dance clubs in the area, including The Hullabaloo in Ann Arbor, The Pumpkin in Westland, and The Inferno in Flat Rock. Located in the Northland Mall in Oakland County, The Mummp was another popular teen club gig. The band once had four different 'managers" at the same time and despite that was reaching a pinnacle. They then signed with Parrot Records, an American division of London Records that had been started in 1964, with several important acts, including The Zombies, Them with Van Morrison, Tom Jones, Lulu, Savoy Brown, Engelbert Humperdinck, and The Moody Blues. "Our grungy Motor City hard rock music achieved another goal when we played the world-famous song three times during 1969 alone," said Stevers. "We're catchin' on!"

With all the success they found, they were on the road constantly. It was far from glamorous, with six guys crammed into a Ford LTD station wagon driving hundreds of miles to get to the next gig. They were making lots of money but had no time to spend it. Although Frijid Pink had played at a slew of Michigan festivals, they spent less time in Detroit after the success of 'House of the Rising Sun,' and the band still suffers from a semi-outsider status in their home town. The band's covers of were unique because instead of trying to imitate the original versions of the tune, the band turned the song inside out by making their own unique version of the song. It was very effective and set the band apart.

The Detroit Vibrations

The original members of the band still jam today. Kelly Green still lives in Michigan, but has had some health issues and recently underwent a quadruple bypass operation; Gary Thompson lives in Grosse Isle and is still playing guitar; Tom Harris is currently playing bass in a covers band and Rick Stevers is very active with gigs around Michigan. Backing vocalists Thelma Hopkins and Joyce Wilson went on to join 'Tony Orlando and Dawn'.

Frijid Pink was voted into the Michigan Rock-n-Roll Hall of Fame in 2013. The band's biggest hit, 'House of the Rising Sun,' was voted a Legendary Michigan Song in 2009.

LINE UP (1967-Present)
Rick Houke - Vocals and Guitar
Brent Austin - Bass and Vocals
Chuck Mangus - Keyboards and Vocals
Rick Zeithami - Lead Guitar and Lead Vocals
Rick Stevers - Drums
Tom Harris - Bass
Jon Wearing - Lead Vocals
Art Wolfe - Lead Guitar
Craig Webb - Guitar and Vocals
Larry Zelenka - Keys

The Detroit Vibrations (1964-1967)
Officially changed its name to Frijid Pink in 1967
Cary, Dayton - Lead Guitar,
Rick Stevers - Drums
Tom Harris - Bass,
Billy O'Reilly - Lead Singer
Tim Machnik - Guitar,
Dan Mason - Keyboards

Band X / The Fendermen

The great white north of Michigan has traditionally not been thought of as a hotbed for creating awesome rock-n-roll bands, but it does happen. Whenever the author has seen Northern Michigan bands, they always seem tighter somehow. "There's really not a lot going on in many areas up here in the winter," said band founder Jay Fortier. "Driving can get treacherous, so the band getting

Band X

together for some serious 'woodshedding' and staying somewhat local is just smart."

Hailing from the Manistee/Luddington area on the west coast of northern Michigan, 'Band X' played all over the state and the midwest during the mid-1960's to the 1970s golden era. They had an agent from Flint who kept them busy on the east side of the state with a very active music scene. Their 45rpm record of 'Rising Sun' was getting decent play in some markets in '68, and they opened for major touring acts. Digging in the vaults, in 2019 an 11-track album 'How Good the Rain' with unreleased tunes from 1968–1969 was discovered and released by Fervor Records of Phoenix.

Band leader Jay Fortier developed an interest in music early on and was exposed to a variety of musical genres as he was growing up in Manistee. Fortier was exposed to live rock through a neighbor who played in an early Manistee band called 'The D-Notes'. However, Fortier's first experience playing in front of a live audience was as part of a folk music trio called The Coachmen. It wasn't long before Fortier used the money he earned from a paper route and mowing lawns to purchase a Gibson Melody Maker electric guitar with a Rickenbacker amp. His buddy Ed Gilbert lined up a Fender Precision Bass soon after and suggested they form a band. Adding Bob Doley on drums and they called themselves 'The Ramrods' after the rocking 1958 instrumental hit by Duane Eddy.

There was only one problem... Doley didn't own a drum set! He solved the problem by "borrowing" two parade snares from the high school marching band room, along with one cymbal that he hung from a garage rafter by a rope with a knot. In the end, he was able to lay down a good drum-back beat. For songs, they were mostly instrumentals by groups like The Ventures, which were very popular at the time. They changed the band name to 'The Magnatones' and became a strictly instrumental group. But the next big change was right around the corner as they realized they now had an all-Fender equipment line-up, so naturally they changed their name to (wait for it)… The Fendermen!

It's important to realize that when they first started to play out as a band, no one in the group even had a driver's license! In those early days, Fortier's parents would most often drive them to gigs in the family van. Doleys remembers that the entire band was paid just $20 at their earliest gigs in Manistee. A year later, they moved up into the $80 to $100 range after they started playing places like the Manistee Rec. Association teen dances. Later, they cut their chops in the recording studio for the first time and their record 'How Good the Rain' was the

#1 single for one week in 1969 on station WTPS-AM in Portage, Michigan, ahead of 'Hey Jude' by The Beatles. Having a record on the radio made a big difference in many ways for the band. "It was kind of a bargaining chip that sometimes helped to get us in the door," said Fortier. "Unfortunately, due to our manager's inexperience, our songs had not been properly registered or identified with ASCAP or BMI, so there were some radio stations that would not play our music."

Local gigs like sock hops and teen dance parties provided a much-needed tune up garage for bands to hone their sound. Indeed, the mid-1960s was the era of teen dance clubs, not just in Detroit but across the state. Band X played at a great number of these clubs across northern Michigan, including The Platters in Cadillac, Paul's Place in Manistee, The Club Ponytail in Harbor Springs, Michigan, The Tanz Haus in Traverse City, The Teen Chalet in Gaylord, Daniel's Den in Saginaw, The Factory in Holland, and The Place in Grand Rapids, just to name a few. They hustled, and the band would also set up their own gigs at the Manistee Armory if they had a free weekend. It wasn't long before Band X was soon opening for acts with national hit singles such as the Shadows of the Knight, the Blues Magoos, and the Box Tops. "My favorite gig of all time was opening for The Blues Magoos at the Windjammer in Kalamazoo in the summer of 1968," said Fortier.

The Band X lineup continued to go through personnel changes over the years, as all bands do. In its many different forms, this was a popular band that was together during the golden era from 1964 to 1972. "We were fortunate to have great support from family and friends, and we were in the right place at the right time," explained guitarist Fortier.

In 1973, the band reformed as 'North Country'. The original concept of the latest name change was to call attention to the region of Michigan that the band comes from rather than signal any new musical direction. They are still out there playing rock-n-roll to the people today, and anyone who heard them back in the day or last week you saw one of the most popular bands in Michigan.

LINE UP 1966-1971
Jay Fortier - Bass, guitar, vocals
Alan Swanson - Guitar, vocals
Jim Toczynski - Keyboards, piano; bass, alto sax
Bob Doleys - Drums
Other Members through the years; Joe King-Drums RIP, Ed Gilbert Bass-Vocals, Dan Hansen Guitar-Cornet-Flute-Vocals RIP, Don Pelarski Bass, Edgar Struble Organ, Valve Trombone, Vocals

Savage Grace

It's been a month of Sundays since Savage Grace played and who remain, to this day, the best and most original live band I have ever heard or seen. I'm lucky; I have the live tapes, or at least some of them, and, to a large extent, they do indeed do the band justice! I saw them at Uncle Russ' Roc-n-Roll Revival at the fairgrounds and at the Birmingham Palladium. But the remaining issue is that they're so damnably unknown to the rest of the world outside Detroit.

Savage Grace

The raves about Koss and Al are numerous because Koss is still one of the best guitar players ever, and Al was the perfect singer/bass player. But folks never mention Larry Zack. and they really should, because Zack was the perfect drummer, and any player will tell you that when you find the perfect drummer, you have struck real gold. Zack, in those days, there could have been so many different kinds of drummers. They could have just picked almost any style and it would have worked. But he didn't tie himself down that way. That's why Jackson Browne kept him so long, because finding a simpatico drummer for David Lindley isn't the easiest audition on the planet.

In the same way as with Ringo... or, it seems, any of them Tulsa drummers... Zack could cook the meat any way you wanted it. or tastefully choose himself if you

Ron Koss

weren't really sure. A very, very overlooked and under-appreciated percussionist who never sought fame and yet got it anyway... His way.

And then, there's Ron... who, I guess, wants to be thought of as an enigma. And he sure as hell is entitled to be... but man, what a player, what a writer.

And then there was the live band... It's easy, of course, to focus on Koss and Jacquez because they were right there, out front. But even a casual listen to any of the Savage Grace live performances is able to decree what a well-integrated four-piece band, not just two upfront guys with a faceless rhythm section. Larry Zack is certainly one of the top five drummers to ever come out of the Midwest, and John Seanor is easily one of the top writers and keyboard players from the same neck o' the woods. And, as a band, the four of them were brilliant arrangers, taking songs and giving them a special feel.

There is an excellent CD made by Savage Grace 3, as they now call themselves, featuring these three superb tracks, featuring the last official guitar tracks by the

Thunder God of Detroit Rock, Ron Koss.

<u>LINE UP</u>

Ron Koss – Guitar & Vocals - RIP
Al Jacquez – Guitar & Vocals
Mark Gougeon - Bass & Vocals
Jeff Jones - Guitar
Bill Gordon - Drums
Jim Claire - Keyboards

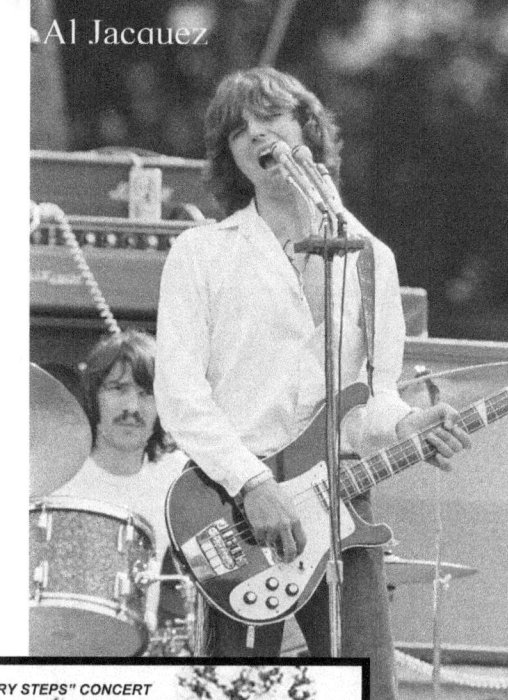
Al Jacquez

!!! *THIRD POWER* !!! @ "THE DETROIT LIBRARY STEPS" CONCERT

The 3rd Power

They were an excellent band that made a name for themselves in the Ann Arbor music scene of that era. Formed in 1967 they had a unique sound that combined elements of rock, blues, and psychedelia. The 3rd Power, known as just 'Third Power', gained some recognition with their high-energy performances and intricate guitar work. They released their self-titled debut album in 1968, which showcased their musical talents and experimental approach. Despite their relative success, which included opening for bands like The Who and Cream, The 3rd Power disbanded in 1970, yet their music lives on.

Although their time together was relatively short-lived, The 3rd Power left a significant impact on the Detroit music scene. Their music continues to be appreciated by fans of '60s rock and psychedelic music. The band gained some recognition with their high-energy performances and intricate guitar work. They released their self-titled debut album in 1968, which showcased their musical talents and experimental approach. Despite their relative success, The group disbanded in 1970. Although their time together was relatively short-lived, The 3rd Power left a significant impact on the Detroit music scene. Their music continues to be appreciated by fans of '60s rock and psychedelic music

LINE UP
Jem Targal - Guitar/Vocals - RIP
Kenny Aaronson - Bass/Vocals
Bob Hames - Drums

Wilson Mower Pursuit
Another local band that gained popularity in the late 1960s was Wilson Mower Pursuit (WMP) from the Royal Oak and Berkely areas. The band was known for their unique blend of soul, rock, and pop music. The name Wilson Mower Pursuit was a double entendre. We told

Wilson Mower Pursuit

our fans that we were a blues band in pursuit of a fictitious bluesman named Wilson Mower, but in reality, how could five middle-class guys ever have the blues? The answer is having to push a Wilson lawn mower on a Saturday afternoon when you would much rather be

Wilson Mower Pursuit

playing baseball with your friends. The only recordings of the group from that era were three songs, two originals, "Lights" and "Noah's Nark Ark" and a traditional folk song previously covered by The Grateful Dead "Cold, Rain and Snow".

As one of the most popular groups in the Michigan area from 1967 to 1968 WMP opened for rock band heavyweights like The Byrds, Procol Harum, B.B. King, and Moby Grape, and on one occasion, they were the headliner when the top act, Soft Machine, failed to show. The first time the band played the Grande they were mistaken for the band Cream because the lead guitarist of WMP, a perfect-pitch musician, had perfectly nailed Clapton's guitar licks, note for note. Although little known throughout the rest of the nation, Wilson Mower Pursuit was among the most popular live bands in their native Detroit during the late 1960s, often playing the famed concert venues of the day including the Grande.

Today, the two founding members, Robert Burwell and Paul Koschtial continue to write and record music for movies and TV.

LINE UP
Robert Allen Burwell - Bass (founding member)
Paul Frank Koschtial - Lead Guitar (founding member)
George **Korinek** / Second Guitar
Dave O'Brien - Lead Singer
Robert J. Franco / Jim Butler - Drums

Scarlet Omen / Highway

Representative of bands that used The Grande and the bands of the late 60's as inspiration, Scarlet Omen's unique blend of rock and alternative sounds, coupled

with powerful and passionate lyrics, garnered them a dedicated fan base back in the day. Originally called 'HighWay' the bands energetic performances and catchy tunes led to their success on the local teen circuit, which was in its death knell for bands as they were slowly replaced by DJs with large PAs and Light Shows playing the hits of the day via records and CDs. They were the cover band's cover band. Scarlet Omen made their small mark on the music scene by playing a large number of dances and proms in the early-mid 1970s. For example, they performed at Southfield, Farmington, Livonia, and Novi High Schools, as well as at special events. "Of course we had always wanted to play the Grande, but we got to the party a little too late. By 1971-72, it was the end of the golden age, and more and more events and venues started using DJs or doing karaoke or comedy," said Lennard. The author was lead vocalist in this band.

LINE UP

Mark Hargraves - Guitar / Vocals
Mark Lennard - Guitar / Vocals
Pete Washburn / Dave Kline - Bass
Tom McAuliffe - Lead Vocals / Harp
Jerry Basil / Joe Kline - Drums

Roseville's own celebrities, the TIDAL WAVES: Mark, Jon, Tom, Bob, and Vic

The Tidal Waves

The Tidal Waves formed in 1964 and had a hit song, 'Farmer John', which was a top 10 song in August of 1966. They followed up with three other top 20 tunes and were considered one of the top mid-Michigan bands, keeping them dancing from Battle Creek to Flint to Lansing and back again. The band was led by Jon Wearing and featured Bob Slap, who produced nearly 40 albums in his career and became the touring guitarist for David Ruffin, the Magic Tones, and the Drifters. In 1967, Bill Long replaced Slap.

"I got my start with a thirty-dollar Champ acoustic guitar, with the strings a half inch off the fretboard, making my fingers almost bleed," Long said. "Eventually, I learned to play well enough to form my own band with friends from Normandy Street in Roseville, Michigan. We called ourselves 'The Logicals' for the combinations of our last names, Long, Gervasi, Kolar, and Kouri. We played local school dances and parties," he said. "I was in ninth grade at Burton Junior High when I joined 'The Tidal Waves'.

The band performing at Ford Auditorium with The Dave Clark Five and at Olympia Stadium with The Animals and Herman's Hermits were highlights. "It was quite a thrill to play for thousands of screaming fans, and to sing through the same Altec Lansing microphones the

Beatles sang through just a few weeks earlier!" Long said. They wrote all their own material and played at the Ballroom with Three Dog Night. "We always loved playing the Grande!" He said.

LINE UP
Tom Wearing - Drums / Vocals
Mark Karpinski - Guitar / Vocals
Bill Long - Guitar / Vocals
Vic Witkowski - Rhythm Guitar / Vocals
Jon Wearing - Percussion / Vocals
Dennis Mills / Bob Slap - Bass

The Bouys

The Bouys were a rock band that played in the Detroit area from 1965 to 1969. They began in early 1965 as The Captives, formed by Tom Cantalini and Ron Bretz, two 8th grade guitar players armed with their fist electric guitars. The band was augmented by two of their St. Monica Elementary School classmates, Tony Turnbull on drums and Mike Gage on bass (after he learned that the ukulele he brought to the first rehearsal was not a bass! "It only has four strings… like a bass!").

The young bandmates played at a few parties in the summer of '65, including one at drummer Tony's house. There, the band met future drummer Scott Satterlund. Even though he had a cast on his forearm, Scott played some drums with the band that night and impressed the band enough to eventually make him a member. Mike Gage left the band when his family moved, and Ron took

over on bass. Ron's older brother, Bob, joined by playing a Farfisa organ. After Mike, Rick Roberts played rhythm.

Finally, the band added Scott's classmate, Bruce Govan, on lead vocals and Ron's classmate, the late Paul LaRose, on rhythm guitar. They completed the sound of the band with Bruce's vocal chops and Paul's spirit and rapidly-developing guitar skills. These six: Tom, Ron, Scott, Bob, Bruce, and Paul, became the band (now known as The Bouys) for most of the band's existence.

By the end of 1966, The Bouys began playing (gigging) regularly around Detroit. They got their start at some of the many Catholic schools in the area. This was no surprise, as all six attended Catholic school. But their success outside of the Catholic school circuit came about mostly because of their new manager and a man who has become their lifelong friend, Carnel "C.V." Mickey. He got the band booked at many of the new teenage nightclubs like Club Hullabaloo, the Shindig, the Chatterbox, Ann Arbor's 5th Dimension and the Birmingham Teen Center, where they opened for Bob Seger. And, of course, there were three gigs at the famed Grande Ballroom, one of those opening for the MC5 (who borrowed one of The Bouys' amplifiers for their Theremin). The Bouys also performed their only single on Robin Seymour's 'Swinging Time' Teen TV show on Windsor CKLW-Channel 9.

Beyond the many gigs and the actual money they earned (typically $100 for the band…total!), The Bouys career highlight has to be winning the 1967 Teenage Fair 'Battle of the Bands' at Cobo Hall. The competition was serious, and The Bouys won out over a number of very good bands from across the state. The prizes included $400 in musical equipment, three hours in recording studio time, a gig at the Silverbell Hideout and the opportunity to appear in the national battle of the bands in Chicago. Despite the passage of time, the band still wants everyone to know that The Hideout stiffed them on the gig! But the band did enjoy their trip to Chicago.

A gig that stands out for the band is opening for the MC5 at the Grande. Before they played, Uncle Russ came into the dressing room with Rob Tyner and Wayne Kramer. They politely asked if they could borrow one of amps for their set. Despite concerns the Bouys agreed.

40 BANDS

Downtown
The Opposing Forces • The Vibrations
The Shifting Sands • Love Syndrome
The Electric Circus • The Sleepwalkers
Worlocks • The Necessary Rhythms

Northland
The Rainy Day Women • Us Guys
The Eccentrics • The Why Men
Bad Company • The Outcry
The Morticians • The Six Pack

Eastland
The Latest Date of Time • The Scops
Milessa Mulch Music Men • The Web
The Manchilds • The Crystal Ship
The Endless Chain
Progressive Movement

Westland
The End • The Undecided
The Unveiled • The Midnight Shift
Renisance • The Spin Outs
The Undecided Cause • Mother Orchus

Pontiac
The Strange Fate • The Paper Sun
Dan Rilly and the Sound Excursion
Kross of the Moon • The Lonely Ones
Pepper and the Shakers
The Bouyes • Part of the Public

Do you know one of these bands? >>>

The band played three times in 1967, before the Grande started booking more national acts. We opened for the MC5, SRC, and the Apostles. The poster for our gig with MC5 appears to be the first full Grande poster designed by Gary Grimshaw. They were the boys next door and were all kids from Catholic high schools. They had the required short hair and also wore suits. When the band hit the stage, the Grande audience was incredulous. 'Who the hell are these straight kids? They look like narcs!' But The Bouys won them over. Even now, more than 50 years later, people are amazed at the bands history.

LINE UP
Ron Bretz - Bass, Vocals
Scott Satterlund - Drums
Bob Bretz - Organ, Vocals
Bruce Govan - Lead Vocals
Tom Cantalini - Guitar
Paul LaRose - Guitar

The Wha?

Sometimes the stars aline and things come together and one achieves history. Such is the case with the first band to play The Grande Ballroom, 'The Wha? Band' from SE Michigan. When another band could not make it Uncle Russ made a call and the band filled in at the very last minute. The band got its

start in 1965. The group's name was inspired by a trip to New York taken by the Demsters and O'Connell where they saw a then-unknown guitarist named Jimi Hendrix performing live at the Greenwich Village club Cafe Wha?, hence the name.

They didn't start there... "My Brother Tom asked me to join the Band and meet Dan O'Connell and then Tasseff and others then joined the Band," said Bob Dempster. Before long the bands was out and about playing for the people. Sounding a little like The Rolling Stones or The Yardbirds. They had the basic showbiz down; a unified look, very good young musicians, a drummer that kept a BEAT, excellent choices in cover material an excellent stage presence. In short order they went from just a 'high school band' to a 'pro' cover band that lasted for years.

The band performed gigs across the state including the world famous Grande Ballroom, Dick Clark's Carnaby Street as well as Fish Fry's Churches, High schools, the Palladium in Birmingham and the Mummp at Northland and many other locations. Playing with other bands like MC 5, Clear Light and Brand X... the bands high-energy performances got people up and dancin in the aisles! "The Grande Ballroom performances were awesome and it was great to be able to flip the strobe light switch!" explained Dempster. "It was a special time and Detroit's spirit of the times was pure Magic."

Every musician has bands they like and listen to for inspiration for The Wha? it was local headliners like Jagged Edge, SRC, The Lourdes and the popular local band called Sky.

One performance that stands out in memory was playin Dick Clark's Caravan of Stars at the State Fairgrounds in the fall of 1966. "This was the big time," he said. "On the bill was 'Gary Lewis & The Playboys', 'Sam the Sham & The Pharaohs' and 'The Yardbirds'." They began to disintegrate in early 1967 when Tasseff was sent off to military boarding school, limiting his involvement to

school breaks. He quit the band that summer but the band

continued. Time marches on, fast forward 50 years and only Dan O'Connell and Bob Dempster are still performing live in SE Michigan. The Wha? Went from being the first or one of the very first bands to play everyone's favorite ballroom to a popular group everyone remembers fondly.

LINE UP
Bob Dempster: Vocals / Tom Dempster: Rhythm Guitar
Dan O'Connell: Bass and Vocals
Tom Tasseff: Lead Guitar
Jon Malkovich: Drums

The Thyme

Hailing from Kalamazoo, Michigan The Thyme was a psychedelic garage rock band which became popular in the late 1960s. The band often opened up for major headliners like Cream, Jimi Hendrix, Janis Joplin and The MC5 at venues like the Grande Ball Room and The Union Street Station among others. The band members had varied interests and a lot of side gigs. Some of the side bands that they played in included; Al Wilmot had The Twang Brothers, Groove Monsters and Love Sum (with Doug

Wagner, Mark White, and Randy Underwood). Steve Vandenberg had Beyond (with Mike Rousch and Bob Reilly). Ralph Cole had The Hitch Hikers, which were the early The Thyme, back when they were in Kalamazoo. The Thyme gained some popularity during the 60s particularly with their songs 'Time of the Season' and 'I Found a Love' which were both very popular. They recorded on Phalanx Records out of Portage, Michigan. Then Thyme and was signed to Ann Arbor based A-Square records for quite some time before disbanding in the early 1970's.

LINE UP
Ralph Cole: Lead Guitar, Sitar, Vocals
Steve Vandenberg: Guitar / Vocals
Ed Linenthal: Drums
Al Wilmot: Bass / Vocals

Girls Inc.

Coming out of the streets of Detroit in the middle late 60s came Girls Inc. an all girl group. This was at a time when it seemed like all male bands were emerging from every garage, basement and backyard in the state. The members found each other on bulletin boards at local music shops and the two guitar players were friends in school. "No one in this group ever felt like they couldn't join the hundreds of bands playing all over the city," said Carol the drummer. Competing agains the guys was a challenge no doubt but the young ladies were up for it

"There were issues at times not being taken seriously as female musicians or being looked at as 'Just cute'

however we were not deterred and it only fueled our efforts," she said. And being in the minority did have its advantages sometimes… for example "one time when they threw a concert for Detroit area musicians Jimi Hendrix was the headliner and because we were in the minority we got front row seats!"

The lineup in the band changed little over the years and the final group from 1967 to 1968 included Jean on Guitar, Diane on Bass, Dawn on organ, Dustee on vocals and Carol on drums. Once members were set they printed

up some business cards, had a photo session and the ladies were set up and raring to go. "We landed with a good manager and we found that, for us, jobs were plentiful and steady," Carol said. "We signed on with Mike Quattro Management as a booking agent and that also helped a lot. Of course all the band members were still in high school so most of the gigs were on the weekends," she said.

Girls Inc. kept busy during the late 60s and there were gigs in Michigan, Ohio, Indiana and all over Canada.

"Most of our gigs were in teen spots including places like; The Crows Nest, The Club, The Birmingham Teen Center (which later became the Palladium), Mount Holly resort, The Pumpkin and many others. The band also had two appearances on TV on 'Swinging Time' with CKLW's Robin Seymour," Carol said. "Sometimes the gigs were for just a single band and other times we open for bands like The Rationals and the Amboy Dukes."

Every band member had the goal of writing our their music and cutting a record. "And of course our ultimate goal was to play the Grande. But not all bands got there and yet like us, still had a lot on interesting gigs, made money and had a great time entertaining the people, she said. As for the style of music? "Girls Inc. played Rock-n-Roll! We played whatever people would dance to we would play," she explained.

The band had a goal of playing the ballroom but ran out of time when it closed in 1972. "Our band didn't get to the Grande but we still had a great trip. The best music came out of this era and while it was challenging being an all women band it was worth the effort and was a great ride," Carol said. "Playing in a band at this time was awesome and we feel it's important that Girls Inc. was a small part of Detroit musical history."

LINE UP
Dawn: Rhythm Guitar/Organ
Dianne: Bass
Dustee: Lead Singer
Jean: Lead Guitar/Vocals
Carol Nems: Drums

The Pyramids
A fascinating band from mid-Michigan in the 1960s was The Pyramids. Although they weren't widely known at the time, they have gained a cult following over the years for their unique blend of surf, rock, and psychedelic music. With their signature instrumental sound, The Pyramids created a sonic landscape that was ahead of its time. Their most famous song is "Penetration," which remains a classic in the surf rock genre. It's always exciting to explore the hidden gems of Michigan music history with bands like The Pyramids!

The Jagged Edge
They were a well-known band and gained popularity with their raw and energetic performances, often described as a mix of garage rock and rhythm and blues. The band was known for their tight musicianship and

catchy tunes, and they were often associated with the 'Motor City Sound' that emerged from Detroit during that era. The Jagged Edge may not be as widely recognized today as some of their counterparts from that time, but they made a significant contribution to the developing music scene of 1960s Detroit.

One by one his bandmates have passed. "I am the last to go.," said Dave "Stoney" Mazur. Looking back, ne recalls many highlights for the band. "Look at those posters on line. Every week was memorable. Every week was a new highlight. And my fondest memories got nothing to do with the gigs, but with the stuff that we did in motels or in basements after the gigs," he said. "I still laugh my ass off when one of those old memories pops into my brain, or I meet an old friend who was at one of those after parties." Mazur has reformed the band with various players and plays gigs across the Detroit Metro area.

Pegasus

They were a popular band from Detroit in the 1960s. The band was formed in 1967, and they gained recognition for their energetic live performances and psychedelic rock sound. Some of their notable members included Ron Selico on drums, Ray "Hungry" Hall on vocals, Bob Thompson on lead guitar, Danny Hernandez on rhythm guitar, and Gene Walker on bass. Pegasus released a few singles during their active years but unfortunately didn't achieve mainstream success. However, they were well-loved within the local Detroit scene.

The Red, White & Blues Band

A prominent band from Michigan in the 1960s RWB was led by some incredibly talented musicians; they played a fusion of blues, rock, and soul music that captivated audiences in the local music scene. The band's energetic

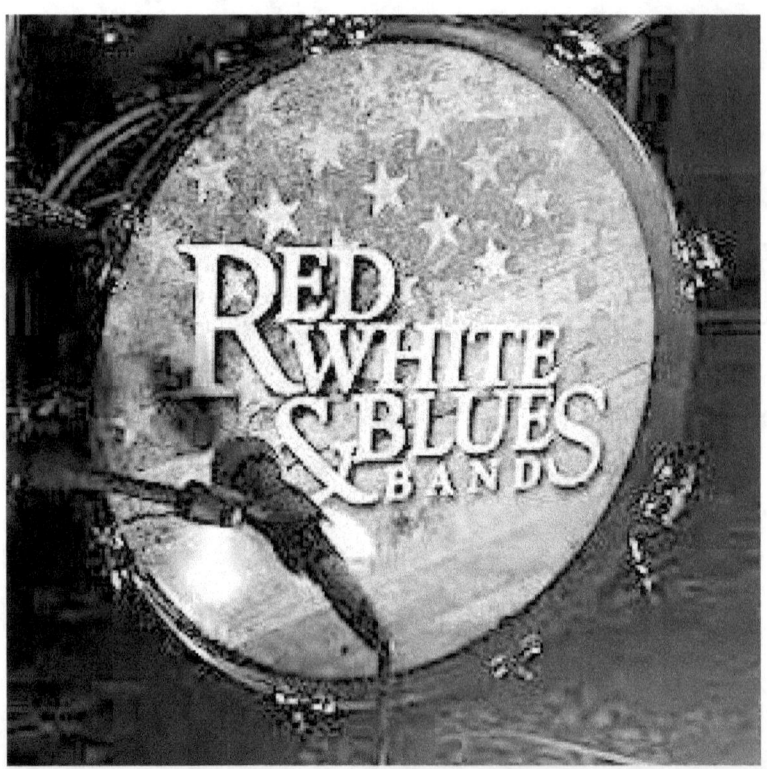

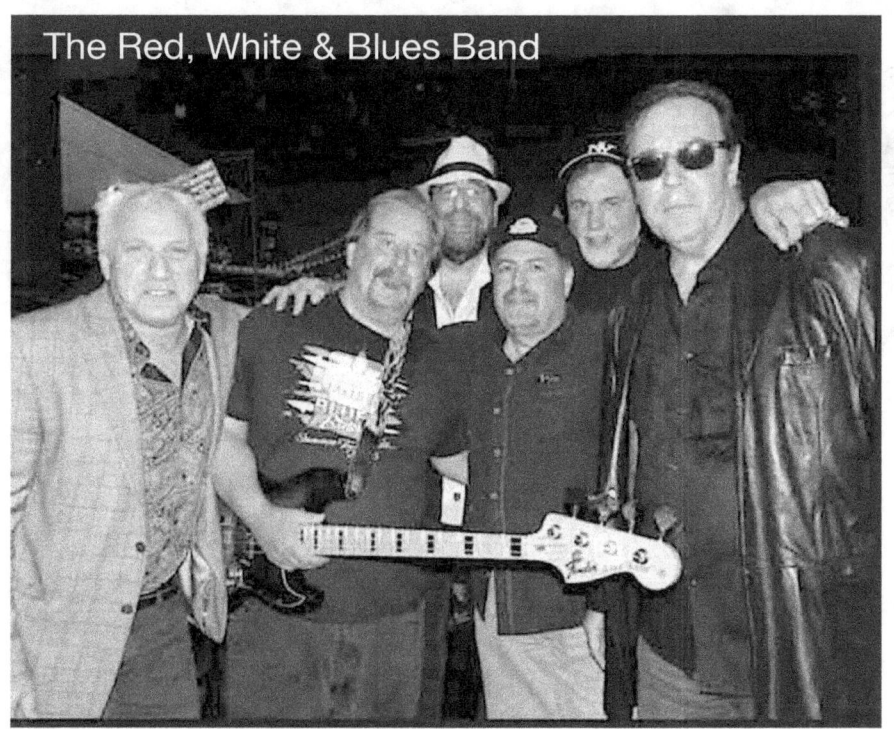
The Red, White & Blues Band

performances and memorable songs made them a favorite among music lovers during that time. Their offerings included rare Chicago and Memphis blues cover tunes and later originals of equal quality. Active from 1966-1972 the band makes music and gigs even today.

The Apostles
Often considered one of the most influential early garage rock bands from Lansing, The Apostles were known for their gritty sound and high-energy performances. They reached regional success with their single 'Stranded in the Jungle' in 1964. R&B, blues, and early psychedelic rock were all present in this band.

The Sunday Funnies / The Daytonas

A band that went by a few different names; First they were known as The Daytonas coming in 2nd Place at the 1964 Michigan State Fair Battle of the Bands. In 1965 Captiol Records changed their name to The Daybreaks and then they morphed into the Psychedelic pop/rockers called The Sunday Funnies. Debuting on Detroit's Hideout record label in 1970 the band released 'Heavy Music' which was well received by fans and local radio. A year later as one of the first groups on Motown's 'Rare Earth' record label they released their self-titled debut LP. The band recorded the album at Motown's Hitsville USA studio, one of the last commercial albums to be recorded

there. 1972 saw the album 'Benediction' as the bands last release. Of note is that England's Andrew Loog Oldham, manager and producer of the Rolling Stones, produced the Sunday Funnies' two albums. Often overlooked they were an important Motor City band both in the early and

late 1960s and early 70s. A engaging live band...they would break up in the mid-seventies.

LINE UP
Richard Fidge - Vocals
Ronald Aitken - Bass/Guitar/Vocals
Richard Kosinski - Keyboards/Vocals
Richard Mitchell /Ross 'Rosco' Helco- Drums
Gary J. Quackenbush - Guitar *(formally with 'SRC')*

These were just some of the regulars at Detroit's Grande Ballroom and they left an indelible mark on popular music although they never achieved widespread fame. Do you know any of them? I, we, loved these bands and

despite perhaps only local success... these artists contributed to the music scene of the city, crafting a sound that was gritty, soulful, and full of energy. They say that the definition of a 'professional' musician is someone who puts $5000 worth of gear into a $500 car to go play a $50 gig. Most musicians and bands are getting about the same rate of pay as the 1970s... $100 a set. And that's not apiece that's total split between 3-4 guys and you can see the reason you don't want your son or daughter to be a musician. Add to that the growing inroads of DJs, the dwindling number of clubs and the coming of push button digital technologies where basically every shithead and their brother can sound decent... it all marked a growing difficulty for live rock.

All in all, the 1960s was the most exciting time for rock music not just in Detroit but across America. Sadly it will not be repeated. The city birthed numerous bands and artists that have left a lasting International impact on the genre and some do so even today. Before very long the 'Detroit Sound' began to spill out and across the country. And it was not just Motown although that music was extremely popular. The music of these little known bands continues to inspire and resonate with us and fans around the world.

Chapter 3

The Communiqués
Keeping the People Informed

'Hey, what's going on? How come you're not burning The Grande down?' And one of the kids said, 'No way! They got music in there, man!'
Interaction outside the Ballroom during the '67 Riots

In any growing community, it's vital to have vehicles for communication. Be it radio, TV, newspapers, or magazines, they allow dialogue on public issues of the day, as well as music, art, and news around town.

Detroit has always had a strong history of mass media. It was one of the first 'two newspaper towns', with an independent morning paper, The Detroit Free Press, and the afternoon paper, The Detroit News. Both papers were hesitant to address, let alone provide significant coverage to, 'a bunch of dirty, long-haired hippies.' In 1966, the paper hired a young British rock journalist to write a column called 'Rock It to Me!' covering the music and art events of the motor city. Other newspapers around the state were slow to follow suit, but by 1969, most dailies had some sort of 'Youth' column.

The 5th Estate underground newspaper and its coverage of Detroit music and where we could go hear it was a conduit to concerts, shops, and events of the pre- and post-Woodstock nation. It was our coconut wireless!

Then there was CREEM. The Magazine quickly became the preeminent rock music magazine in America. In 1969, the monthly magazine was taken over by local

businessmen Barry Kramer. It gained popularity for its irreverent and often humorous approach to music, politics and the growing youth culture. CREEM was America's only true rock-n-roll magazine. It was the springboard for many top rock journalists, from the wry Dave Marsh and flame-throwing Lester Bangs, both editors over the years, to stellar writers like Greil Marcus. CREEM became known for its passionate and independent coverage of rock music, be it artist features, concert or album reviews or features on the issues of the day. In addition, it was the first major publication to embrace rock genres like punk and heavy metal. It featured renowned music writers like Bangs, who became famous for his fearless and provocative writing style. Although the publication eventually faced financial difficulties and ceased publication in 1989, its impact on music journalism and its legacy as a unique and influential voice in rock music remained significant. The magazine was resurrected as an online ePub in 2021.

During the 1960s and 1970s, there were several underground newspapers in Michigan that emerged as part of the counterculture movement. But the most notable publication was called "The Fifth Estate." It was a radical and alternative newspaper that provided a platform for independent voices and covered topics such as anti-war activism, civil rights, feminism, and environmentalism, among many others. The Fifth Estate was well known for its criticism of mainstream politics and its willingness to challenge societal norms. It played a significant role in the alternative media landscape of Detroit during that special time. It is still published today.

♪

VENUES

THE GRANDE BALLROOM
THE EASTOWN
THE CAROUSEL BALLROOM
THE PALLADIUM
20 GRAND
THE HIDEOUT
WESTSIDE 6
THE PUMP
THE CHATTERBOX
CLUTCH CARGOS
BOOKIES
THE TIP TOP CLUB
THE CROWS NEST
THE SILVERBELL
SOMETHING DIFFERENT
HULLABALOOS
THE PUMPKIN
& MANY MORE!

CHAPTER 4

The Clubs
A Place to Play, a Place to Dance

"We survived on playing Teen Clubs, school Dances it provided a wonderful training ground for us while putting money in our pockets."
Guitarist Mark Lennard, Scarlet Omen

There were tons of places to party, dance, talk and 'experience'. The Hideout was a popular teen nightclub in Detroit in the 1960s. It was located on Vernor Highway and was known for its live music performances, particularly featuring local rock and soul bands. There was also one in Redford. While its not full documented it is believed that by 1969-70 there were at least 7 or 8 'Hideouts' across the state. The venue provided a platform for emerging musicians and bands to showcase their talent and build a following. It was a favorite spot for young people to gather, dance, and enjoy live music. It played a crucial role in developing the local music scene and contributed to the vibrant culture of Detroit.

During this time the greater metro area had several high schools that played significant roles in providing a place for these bands to play. Here are a few notable high schools from that time:

Cass Technical High School
Located in Cass neighborhood the school has a long history and is known for its strong academic and arts

programs. It has produced many distinguished alumni, including Motown label musicians and artists.

Catholic Central High School
A prominent all-boys Catholic high school located in Novi, Michigan. It has a strong academic reputation and offers a rigorous college prep curriculum. It featured dances or events where bands were booked, twice a month. Students could attend if their grades were good!

Mumford High School
Mumford High School is known for its diverse student body and strong athletic programs. It has produced many successful graduates for the NBA, NFL and MLB.

Pershing High School
Pershing High School near Hamtramck, has a rich history and excels in academics, athletics, and the arts. For dances instead of the gym where the acoustics were horrible they had another huge room and would put up a

wooden dance floor.

Southfield High School

SHS has been serving the community since 1951. It offers a comprehensive education and has a strong commitment to alternative education according to materials. They had bands playing almost every week and amazingly the world famous band 'The Who' from the UK, played there in 1967. Tickets were $4.50!

These are just a few examples of the many high schools in the Detroit area during the 1960s. There were many more that played a significant role in shaping the lives of students during that time and more importantly a place for rock musicians to play and 'get good'.

In the 1960s, Michigan also had dozens of teen clubs where young people could gather, socialize, and dance

TEEN CLUBS

The Hideout (several clubs)
Birmingham Teen Center
Cage Au-Go-Go
Walled Lake Casino
Greenlawn Grove
Wamplers Lake Pavilion
The Fifth Dimension
Crow's Nest - 2 clubs
The Chatterbox
The By-Pass
Evergreen Amusment Park
Mt. Holly Resort
Something Different
The Inferno
Hullabaloo's (multiple clubs)
The Pumpkin
The Mummp
The Club
The Top Hat
Blue Light -Midland
BMF Club
Boblo Island Boats
Double O, Traverse City
Plain Brown Wrapper, Grand Rapids
The Sceen, Sunfield-Lake Odessa
The Cobra Club, Hastings
Teen Inc., Battle Creek
The Note, Yankee Springs
and tons more!

while listening to live music. Some popular teen clubs:

The Factory: Located on Gratiot Avenue, The Factory was a popular spot for teenagers to hang out and enjoy live music. It showcased local bands and provided a platform for them to perform. Cover charge was $1.

The Eastown: The legendary venue on played a significant role in rock-n-roll. It hosted many famous rock acts of the era, such as The Who, The Doors, Led Zeppelin, Pink Floyd and more.

Cinderella Ballroom: Situated on Woodward Avenue, the Cinderella Ballroom was another well-known venue for live music in the 1960s. It hosted various local and national acts, including popular Motown artists.

The Roostertail: Located on East Jefferson Avenue near Belle Isle. The Roostertail was primarily a nightclub but also hosted select teen club events on the weekends. It featured live bands and provided a space for young people to dance and socialize.

The People's Ballroom: In Ann Arbor just off the University of Michigan campus the venue was started by John Sinclair and featured most of the same bands that played the Grande and other venues in Detroit. They would sometime have FREE nights with no cover charge.

These are just a few examples, but there were so many other teen clubs and venues that catered to the musical tastes and social needs of teenagers.

These teen dance clubs, where alcohol was not served and "garage bands" were the norm was not just in the big city of Detroit but in small towns too. The Sceen (Sunfield-Lake Odessa) near Grand Ledge was a major venue during this time and showcased local bands. But there were many other clubs in the mid-Michigan area. The Sceen (not the Scene) hosted several local bands including; Tonto and the Renegades from and the Beaux Jens The Sceen was also home turf of the Lavender Hill Mob band. The "Cobra Club" in Hastings, Michigan was located at the site of the Roll-A-Rama. In addition to local bands groups like Bob Seger and Canned Heat preformed there. Elsewhere Battle Creek had a couple of clubs such as "Teen Inc." and "Eddy's". There was also a club called 'The Note' on Duck Lake near Traverse City.

The Incline Club was located in downtown Lansing across from the Community College. And across town 'The Hullabaloo Club', was located at Logan St. and West Jolly, the current site of the Déjà vu Club. The club was a knock-off from 'The

Hullaballoo Show', a TV musical variety and dance program that was cancelled in 1966. The Washington Street Armory downtown, was the scene of frequent 'Battle of the Bands' with winners taking home the prize money of a whopping $75!

The Detroit / Ann Arbor area by itself supported hundreds of bands with hundreds more spread across the great white north within a hierarchy of clubs and concert venues that existed no where else. The resulting scene created numerous bands that could wipe the stage with the best national recording/touring acts of the time. The allure of smaller teen clubs faded as Detroit's legendary concert halls like the Grande Ballroom and the Eastown rose to prominence and became the goal for many bands.

The music scene during that time was bustling with so many venues and talented bands, it's easy to see and not uncommon for some bands, in fact most bands to have remained relatively obscure. The golden era of the Detroit music scene was bustling with so many talented bands we thought it would go on forever, but change was in the winds and in the 1970s when the drinking age was lowered to 18 years old and with the advent of DJs and Karaoke, the scene changed almost overnight and was virtually wiped out.

CHAPTER 5
The Records Go Round and Round
The Strangle Hold of Record Companies on Detroit Rock-n-Roll

"I don't care about being on a label. I just want to make this music and then find a way to get it out there to the people."
Dick "The Maestro of Rock" Wagner

Record companies have always been about money and for as far back as the 1940's the recording industry as always turned a blind eye to Detroit music. That was especially true with Rock acts. Long before MP3's and online music small local record stores were how the big Record companies got the music to the fans.

In the 1960s, Detroit was a vibrant and influential hub for the music industry, particularly known for its thriving independent record companies. The most prominent example is Motown Records, founded by Berry Gordy Jr. in 1959. Although Motown gained significant national and international success by the 1960s, it began as an independent record company in Detroit. The label's success paved the way for other independent record companies to flourish. Independent labels such as United Sound Systems, Westbound Records, and Grande Records emerged to support artists in rock-n-roll.

One example of a successful Michigan record label is Fortune Records, founded by Jack and Devora Brown in the 1950s. Fortune Records initially specialized in country and blues recordings but later expanded into rock and roll and pop. They released music by artists like John Lee Hooker. There were also other smaller independent labels, such as Golden World Records, Thelma Records, and Carla Records, that emerged. Holland started A2 Records in Ann Arbor; Punch Andrews started his own record label, as did almost anyone with a pulse. These labels, although not as commercially successful as Motown, still played a crucial role in nurturing local talent and releasing rock music with a distinct Detroit sound to the world.

In recent years, smaller independent record companies have played a crucial role in showcasing Detroit's rock bands. Labels like Third Man Records, founded by Jack White of The White Stripes, have helped support and promote local rock bands, keeping the spirit of Detroit's rock scene alive. In addition to Motown, other record companies, both local and national, played a part in promoting Detroit rock bands. For instance, Atlantic Records signed the politically charged and influential Detroit rock band known for their high energy, the MC5. To get in on the act Motown started its 'Rare Earth Records' rock division. Another important record label was Elektra Records, which signed and showcased bands like The Stooges and Alice Cooper.

Overall, independent record companies in Detroit during the 1960s were instrumental in shaping the city's musical landscape, producing influential artists and releasing their music to the masses across the world and contributing to the soul, R&B, and rock music coming out of the mitten state with most bands eventually having their own label.

The stranglehold that corporations like RCA and Capitol, held was broken by innovators like Berry Gordy of Motown and dozens of other smaller independent producers and recording labels. As the technology improved and became increasingly affordable, more and

more local bands put their talents on vinyl, with varying degrees of success. Radio air play for most Detroit rock acts was limited despite the public's appetite for it. Local bands found that it was one thing to make a record but it was quite another to get it played on the radio air waves.

Foremost among the record company's of the era is Motown. Its success was built on a unique sound that blended pop, soul, and R&B, making it a cultural phenomenon that left a lasting impact on the music industry. But aside from Motown, there have been other influential record companies in Detroit. Independent labels such as United Sound Systems, Westbound Records, and Grande Records emerged to support artists in various genres, including funk, rock, and punk. Back in the day Detroit rock bands, such as Grand Funk Railroad and The Amboy Dukes did have successful partnerships with record companies. Grand Funk Railroad, signed to Capitol Records, achieved mainstream success in the early 1970s with hit songs like "We're an American Band" and "Some Kind of Wonderful." Similarly, The Amboy Dukes, fronted by Ted Nugent, had a successful run with their record company, Mainstream Records, in the late 1960s. So did Seger with Hideout Records.

While record companies have had a significant role in promoting and supporting artists, there have been instances of greed and exploitation within the industry. Greed can manifest in various ways, such as unfair contracts, exploitative practices, and prioritizing profits over the well-being of artists. Overall, the issue of greed in record companies is a complex and ongoing one. As the music industry continues to evolve, it's crucial for all stakeholders, including artists, record companies, and consumers, to push for fairness, transparency, and ethical practices that prioritize the well-being and success of the artists we know and those we don't. As their music is rediscovered these Michigan bands of the golden era of the 60s deserve fair and just compensation.

CHAPTER 6

A2 - The Ann Arbor Connection
Jeep - like the Car,
Holland - like the Country...

'Jack of all trades... master of none?'
Old Saying

When one first walked into his office...the back room of a one bedroom apt in Ann Arbor in 68... he would be trimming tiny pieces of laminate from around a passport sized photo of Dave Clark of the Dave Clark Five band.... Each small sliver of extra laminate was lovingly placed into position on a two column-inch newspaper clipping from the New Musical Express. Gradually the picture could comfortable yield no more spare laminate... and he quietly picked up another untrimmed picture Billy J Kramer and the Dakotas and continued his painstaking work. His phones rang incessantly... mostly from an angry Dick Wager who kept saying.. "I know yer there dammit, pick up the phone..."

At the time, Frost was high on the list of A2 acts.. a stable that contained bits of the careers of all, some or none of depending on who ya believe Rationals, Third Power, Frost, Jagged Edge, Wilson Mower Pursuit, Scott Richards Case, Amboy Dukes, Bob Seger, The Woolies, MC5, Stooges, Thyme... and every other worthwhile musician in a two hundred mile radius.

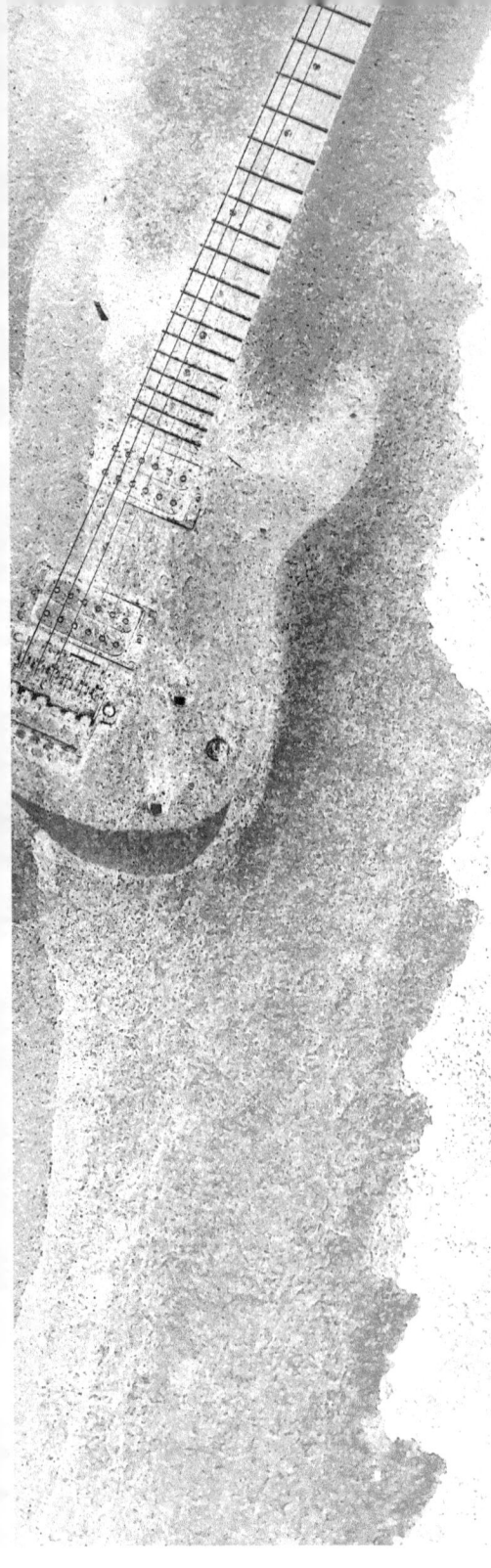

"Jeep Holland was a really smart guy. He had been studying Latin in school, and he just wanted to be a bohemian, I think. He just wanted to drop out. But he was very intelligent. So he applied some pretty smart tactics to his projects," explained Scott Morgan of The Rationals and the popular band SRC. "He was also kind of a megalomaniac... he wanted to do everything. He wanted to be the Manager, the Producer, a Booking Agent... do it all. He had a little trouble giving any of that up to anybody else," Morgan said. "He was good at it all though, it just kind of became too much. He wanted to control everything and after a while, it's too much. You can't do it all!" Wanna bet?

There were people sleeping in the outer room... upright in chairs and drooling... there were stacks of burger and soda debris.. there were more phone calls. people who stuck in a tentative head and left immediately... It was bedlam in the courtyard of the king.

He was juggling more balls than levity and gravity would allow. There were draftees to help avoid service, recordings to be mixed, records to be pressed and promoted, bands and clubs to be booked, a staggering array of correspondence to be answered or initiated, on subjects as diverse as mechanical royalties and Cher's ass or lack of it... to local politics. The battle lines were drawn, and then moved by A2 and it's many ship-jumpers to that college town. For that is how they were seen and described. Those who rode the A2 bus to their own stop and then got off. The Five, Pete Andrews ex partner, Punch, Russ, Wagner, Scott Morgan, Iggy....

Through the front door of 521 North Division came the mess of humanity that would form and formulate much of what has come to pass in the last years - goin' on fifty. Even more significant within his own web than Bill Graham was in his - the engine, transmission, steering and brakes of the rock-n-roll chopper that led America into the 70s and beyond came out of those small rooms.

THE STORY OF MICHIGAN'S LEGENDARY A-SQUARE RECORDS

(OF COURSE)

Featuring MC5 THE SCOT RICHARD CASE THE THYME THE PRIME MOVERS THE APOSTLES THE UP and more

BIG BEAT

When faced with a kaleidoscope of memories, all of which seem to intermingle frequently, it is difficult to find an end thread to begin unravelling according to those who were there.

Hugh Henry Jeep Holland was as complex a person as brute simplicity would allow... a staggering mental gymnast with deplorable organization skills, he dealt his hands with the twin indomitable forces that carved, not just a career but a untold legend of passion and obstinance. Bull headed and bull hearted he would add another cause to champion to his roster without regard for what the effect would be. He might find a kid who helped hump sound systems at gigs, just to be around the scene.. and he would "adopt" the kid... nourish his ego and bathe him in a rare sense of self confidence.. he would make phone calls and cajole friends and colleagues alike until the kid had an actual job...within the industry. And the industry took Jeep's word as a world class talent assessor.

Unfortunately, the time and effort spent on the phone calls sometimes took away from that needed to organize a rehearsal hall for last week's cause celebre. He would make it up with the "borrowing from Peter" system, but like all pyramid schemes it was doomed to fall apart eventually - unless he could find an assistant. But the assistant had to have the same passions.. the same fluctuating ethics...the same fire, knowledge, ego, optimism and loathing for silly badges. And the assistant also had to be willing and able to have all his own hard work undone by Jeep's vagaries and unpredictability -

without taking it personally. And there were many of them... bright, energetic, powerful people who could have effectively gone it alone.. but in those days, we all needed a barometer to show the way.. Jeep just tracked by the stars and the muse…and he was never ever wrong.

Look at the talent that he spotted and nurtured, and consider what music and particularly Michigan Rock-n-Roll would have been if such talent had been left ignored. In addition he guided and argued Russ into booking the headline Grande acts...he was the main booking act for Silverbell, Hideout, Palladium, the Mummp, and most of the high schools in the area. He produced the best of the Michigan popfests... no-one else would have thought to put Sun Ra and the Bonzo band together. His booking agent hat alone should get him a statue in Ann Arbor.

And then there was the label… A2 Records…creating, producing, mixing... matching the song to the act and getting the best out of them on the day… if Jeep had never done anything else except to bring us The Rationals version of 'I need you' his place in the history of international blue-eyed soul would have been assured. Given today's technology it could certainly sound better, cleaner...maybe -but it was Jeep that picked the song, Jeep that allowed Scott Morgan to rip the lining out of his soul in the studio... and Jeep knew how to mix it hot for A.M. radio. In addition to that classic, the Rats and Thyme between them made beautiful hit-quality vinyl under the tutelage and taste of the energetic - some might say frantic - Jeep. The tapes that Jeep produced and recorded for A2 still lurk unreleased.

Then there was his management style...although often unofficial which caused many problems down the line apiece it was artist management after the style of a personal manager. Jeep wasn't any good at the disciplines of finances... he had the brilliance to know how to get to where he wanted to go but where he wanted to go wasn't always the best move, from a business standpoint. And thank heaven...

It made horrific business sense to fund... or co-sign - or borrow equipment for bands that were often little more than high school kids, but between Jeep and Al Nally.. and even Russ on occasion there were an awful lot of Fender amps and Guitars floating around Michigan with precious little financing. Eventually Sunn amplifiers got themselves linked up with Jeep and then, before ya could set the volume up to eleven, the amps stood on most of Michigan's stages and many in Ohio and Illinois as well.

Jeep was largely responsible for the Free Concerts in the park in Ann Arbor. And then there were the draft dodge stories. One doubts if many of those involved would admit to such goings-on nowadays... being kept up for 48 hours on a diet of coffee and crosses, no washing or underwear changes for a week, dropped-off at the local draft board and consequently being declared 4F- and allowed to return to the subversive world of rock-n-roll... this never really happened... did it? Yer damn fuckin' a right it happened... time after time... It was the Jeep system. After the draft lottery came in, the system faded away but by then it's function was accomplished. And then there was talent galore that needed direction and promotion…

Singers? We had Scott, Rob, Seger, two Stoneys, Catfish, Mitch, Wagner, Targel, Jacquez...

Drummers? How about Johnny B, Pep Perrine, Teegarden, Larry Zack, Optner..Iggy even...

Bass Players? Yep! Hartman, Jacqez, Treband, Feiger, English, Skip Vanwinkle's feet..

The list goes on and on.. horns, harps, keyboards... the Motor City had 'em all.. and they all played, everywhere, every week and most nights. They played in High Schools, and VFW Halls...teen clubs and parking lots...they became an unstoppable force, and they took their audiences with them from gig to gig. I went to see and hear them all... well as many as I could! And everywhere I went.. there were the tell-tale fingerprints and footprints of the Jeepster... like Holmes' Moriarty he had fingers in every pie - and every pie tasted better for it. He didn't like to drive and anyone that ever rode shotgun knew why... but his web encircled a tri-state area and his enthusiasm nurtured it as it grew beyond control.

If God himself had showed up at 1am on Sunday morning, Jeep would tell him that he had worn the wrong shirt! But, as he always did, he'd also tell him that he played brilliantly–better than ever before. Jeep was a football coach to Rock-n-Roll, perfecting his Gipper speech until everyone came to believe it. And we did!

CHAPTER 7

Power to the People
Music, Pot and Politics

"The Revolution will not be Televised!"
Gill Scott Herron

Sinclair and the rise of politics in rock-n-roll with the MC5 and its flag burning ways brought a backlash from middle America. The music of Detroit and the anti-war movement became one in the same.

However, Detroit also faced off on significant challenges during this time. The city experienced racial tensions and the Civil Rights Movement had a profound impact. In 1967, Detroit faced one of its most tumultuous periods when the city erupted in riots that lasted for days, resulting in widespread destruction and loss of life. These events brought attention to the underlying racial and socioeconomic disparities that plagued the city, and they continue to be large part of Detroit's narrative to this day.

The 1960s were a pivotal time for a city defined by both prosperity and struggles. It remains an important period to study and understand the city's rich history and its impact on American society. Its easy to see where the conflict would arise from. While the nation was dealing with the war with its sons and daughters coming home in boxes there was also racial tensions in cities across America including Detroit, add to that dope smoking radical John Sinclair and the MC5 screaming 'Kick out the Jams Motherfuckers!' and burning the American flag, however symbolic, did not sit well with the majority of Americans, no matter what their political leanings. Is it any wonder why there was such blow back against the Grande, the bands, the music, the hair… the whole ball of wax? And the response was visceral and immediate both in the public square and in families across the country. The Detroit anti-war movement was a significant grassroots phenomenon that emerged during the late 1960s and early 1970s. Rock music played a crucial role in voicing opposition to the Vietnam War and challenging the government's policies and its enforcement.

One of the primary catalysts for the anti-war movement in Michigan was the growing disillusionment among young people with the government's handling of the war. The draft, which compelled young men to serve in the military, fueled resentment and resistance. Activists, like Sinclare, argued that the war was unjust, based on false premises and that it disproportionately affected the black and marginalized communities who were drafted. This sentiment resonated strongly with African Americans in Detroit, who already faced significant racial inequality and saw their communities devastated by crime and poverty. Demonstrations and protests were a common sight during this period, with large-scale marches taking place in downtown Detroit. The author remembers one protest where we encircled the Military Induction Center joined hands and tried to levitate it off the ground!

The struggle to decriminalize marijuana was also a front-burner issue for most young people at the time (and this was way before legalization like today). Stories of people being put away for life for an ounce of the evil weed were commonplace at the time. As this is written to date, 25 states have legalized cannabis for personal use.

A major tool in changing the public and youth opinion about the war and pot was music. More than any other weapon in the anti-war arsenal was the power and influence of popular entertainers, who increasingly not only spoke out about the war but also wrote songs about it. Who can forget tunes like Marvin's 'What's Goin On?' or 'For What's Worth' by Buffalo Springfield? The power of grassroots activism motivated by and through music helped to show the importance of group dissent in shaping public policy.

One prominent example is the protest song 'War' by Edwin Starr, released in 1970. With its powerful lyrics and intense delivery, the song resonated strongly with anti-war sentiments and became an anthem of the movement. Artists like Bob Dylan and Joan Baez also used their music to call for peace and rally against the war. Songs like 'Give Peace a Chance' by John Lennon and 'Fortunate Son' by Creedence are just a few examples of songs that influenced public opinion about the war.

Music played a significant role in the anti-war movement. It served as a powerful medium for expressing dissent, spreading peace, and rallying

individuals against the war. Musicians and artists used their songs to share stories, evoke emotions, and critique the war effort, helping to shape public opinion and mobilize action and protests. While it is difficult to measure the direct impact of music on ending the Vietnam War, it undoubtedly played a crucial role in shaping public discourse, fostering opposition, and amplifying the voices of those who opposed the conflict in Southeast Asia and wanted to bring the troops home.

Fightin' in the Streets!

On July 23, 1967, the worst event in Michigan history was happening right around the corner from my house. It was the first time many can remember actually feeling unsafe. In total, the 'uprising' lasted five days with 43 deaths, 1,189 injuries, and more than $350 million in business and property damage. Even today, the events of the early morning hours of that hot July night when a police raid on an after-hours Bar exploded into the Detroit rebellion are etched in people's minds.

1967 Detroit Riot Stats
43 Deaths
1,189 Injured
7,200+ Arrests
400+ buildings destroyed
$350+ million in loses

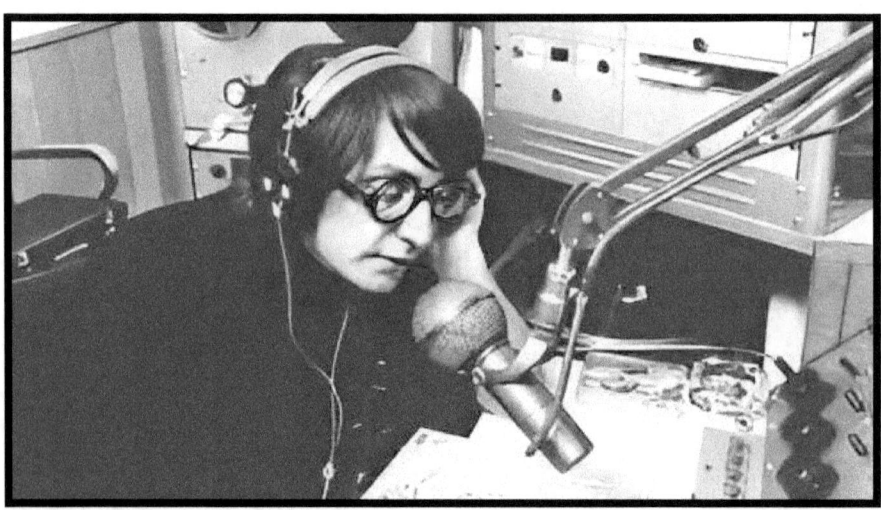

CHAPTER 8
WABX Air Aces and Detroit Radio

"The world was on 10 - the Grande was on 11!"
Alice Cooper

The 1960s was a remarkable era for American radio, and few regions encapsulated the spirit of this decade quite like Detroit. Local radio stations played a significant role in shaping not only the musical landscape of the city but also its cultural fabric. The city's automotive industry dominance provided the perfect breeding ground for a burgeoning rock and soul music scene. Detroit radio acted as a conduit, bringing this unique blend of rhythm and blues, rock-n-roll, and Motown soul sounds directly into people's homes and cars.

One of the most iconic radio stations of the era was WKNR, commonly referred to as 'Keener 13'. Running from 1956 to 1980, this station had a powerful 50,000-

watt signal that reached far beyond the mitten down into America's heartland to as far away as Kentucky.

Another influential station, was all the way from Windsor Canada! Nicknamed 'The Big 8', CKLW was a Top 40 AM powerhouse throughout the decade. It embraced the emerging rock-n-roll movement, playing hits by iconic artists from The Beatles to The Beach Boys. With its catchy jingles, vibrant on-air personalities, and contests, CKLW- AM became a part of Detroiters' daily routines.

Two other stations deserve serious mention; WXYZ, which later became the album rock power station WRIF-FM and WABX 99FM and its 'ABX Air Aces which virtually wrote the book on alternative rock radio with

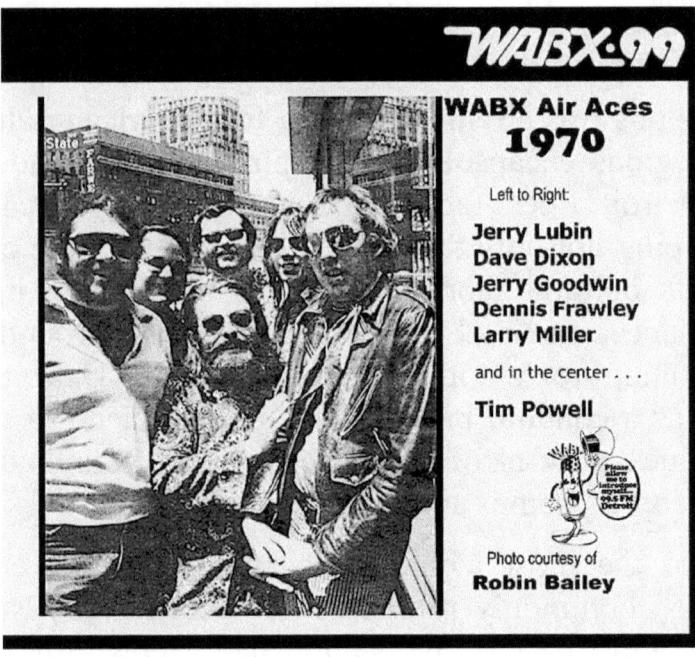

the most community support than of any radio station before or since. In addition to the radio stations themselves, the DJs behind the microphone played a crucial role in shaping the listening experience. Legendary on-air personalities like Dick Pertain, Doug Podel, Arthur Penhollow and Robin Seymour became local celebrities, connecting with listeners on a personal level and creating a bond that extended beyond the airwaves and just having fun addressing themes of racial equality, social justice and alternative lifestyles.

Detroit radio in the 60s, before the computers took over, was more than just a medium for broadcasting music and ads. It was a cultural force, introducing the world to the Motown sound and Detroit Rock-n-Roll. Its legacy lingers to this day, reminding us of the power of radio to connect communities, entertain, inform, sell and helping to transcend social barriers. Sadly 'personality radio' is all but dead and replaced by a computer generated playlist with canned (prerecorded) stop sets spilling time and temp. Call in requests? Surely you jest!

It was an exciting time for music and broadcasting. Detroit has a rich musical history, especially when it comes to the Motown sound. Many iconic artists and groups, such as Stevie Wonder, Marvin Gaye, The Supremes, and The Temptations, emerged from the Motown record label based in Detroit during this era.

In the 1960s, radio played a crucial role in showcasing this music and connecting with the community. Stations like WJBK, CKLW, and WKNR were popular during this

WKNR

DETROIT

MUSIC GUIDE

WEEK OF JUNE 27, 1968

1. JOURNEY TO THE MIND—AMBOY DUKES.....MAINSTREAM (2)
2. THIS GUY'S IN LOVE WITH YOU—HERB ALPERT.......A & M (1)
3. YUMMY YUMMY YUMMY—OHIO EXPRESS...........BUDDAH (3)
4. HURDY GURDY MAN—DONOVAN..............................EPIC (10)
5. LADY WILLPOWER—UNION GAP.........................COLUMBIA (9)
6. GRAZING IN THE GRASS—HUGH MASEKELA..............UNI (11)
7. PICTURES OF MATCHSTICK MEN—STATUS QUO.....CADET (13)
8. THE LOOK OF LOVE—SERGIO MENDES......................A & M (5)
9. INDIAN LAKE—COWSILLS ....MGM (6)
10. REACH OUT OF THE DARKNESS—FRIEND & LOVER...VERVE (4)
11. JUMPIN' JACK FLASH—ROLLING STONES ....LONDON (7)
12. I LOVE YOU—PEOPLE...CAPITOL (14)
13. HERE COME DA JUDGE—BUENA VISTAS ....MARQUEE (8)
14. Folsom Prison Blues—Johnny Cash..................Columbia (26)
15. Stoned Soul Picnic—5th Dimension......................Soul City (22)
16. Stop—Lonette ....M-S (20)
17. Sunday Morning 6:00 A.M.—Camel Drivers.........Top Dog (19)
18. Give Me One More Chance—Wilmer & Dukes....Aphrodisiac (25)
19. If I Only Knew Then—Jimmy Soul Clark ....Moira (18)
20. Rollin' Across My Mind—Peppermint Trolley.............Acta (21)
21. A Place—Precisions ....Drew (23)
22. Down In Tennessee—Kasenetz-Katz Circus..........Buddah (27)
23. Dreams Of Everyday Housewife—Glen Campbell....Capitol (31)
24. I'm A Midnight Mover—Wilson Pickett...................Atlantic (29)
25. Turn On Your Love Light—Bill Black..............................Hi (28)
26. Hitch It To The Horse—Johnny "C"............Phil L.A. Soul (30)
27. Soul Meeting—The Soul Clan.................................Atlantic (KS)
28. Classical Gas—Mason Williams......................................W-7 (HP)
29. Hello I Love You—Doors...Elektra (HP)
30. Breaking Down The Walls—Bandwagon....................Epic (HP)
31. Tuesday Afternoon—Moody Blues..........................Deram (HP)

KEY SONG OF THE WEEK
PEOPLE GOT TO BE FREE—THE RASCALS......................ATLANTIC

( ) Indicates last week's position   (HP) — Hit Preview

Dan Henderson
afternoons
12 Noon – 3 PM

PRINTED IN U.S.A.

time. WKNR, also known as 'Keener 13', gained a significant following with its Top 40 format and energetic flame throwing on-air personalities.

These radio stations heavily promoted Motown artists and helped popularize their music across the country. But they also provided a platform for local rock talent and fostered a sense of culture and community in Detroit. It was a time when DJs were influential figures, and listeners eagerly tuned in to catch their favorite songs, discover new music, and hear the latest news and gossip.

The 1960s also saw the rise of rock 'n' roll and the British Invasion, which introduced bands like The Beatles, The

Rolling Stones, and The Who to American audiences. Detroit radio stations played a pivotal role in bringing this new music to the masses and contributing to the cultural shifts happening across the country.

Detroit radio in the 1960s was a vibrant and dynamic force, shaping the musical tastes of a generation and establishing a legacy that continues to influence the music industry today. The Detroit radio scene in the 1960s was not just about Motown, but it also encompassed a wide range of music genres, including rock, pop, R&B, and soul. The DJs and radio stations played a pivotal role in shaping the musical landscape of the city and beyond.

One notable Detroit radio station of the time was WXYZ, which later became WRIF. It was known for its popular shows like "Swingin' Time" hosted by Robin Seymour, featuring live performances by both local and national acts. The show gave exposure to various artists, including many Motown acts, and helped build their fanbase.

Another influential radio station was WKNR-AM (Keener 13), which had a Top 40 format and was known for its high-energy and fast-paced broadcasts. The station employed charismatic DJs like Tom Shannon and Robin Sherwood, who became household names in Detroit. Keener 13 produced exciting music charts that showcased the most popular songs of the week, contributing to the local music scene's buzz.

CKLW, a 50k watt powerhouse across the Detroit River in Windsor, Ontario, Canada also had a significant impact on the Detroit radio scene. Known as "The Big 8," CKLW played a mix of pop, rock, and Motown hits. Its powerful signal reached a vast audience, even extending as far south as Kentucky, making it a major player.

Apart from the radio stations, many DJs became beloved personalities who kept listeners entertained with their witty banter, music knowledge, and the occasional on-air contests. These DJs were influential trendsetters, often shaping the tastes of their dedicated fans.

Overall, the Detroit radio scene in the 1960s was an exciting and vibrant part of the city's cultural fabric. It played a crucial role in promoting local talent, exposing listeners to new music from different genres, and fostering a sense of community. The impact of Detroit radio on the music industry during this era continues to reverberate today, leaving a lasting legacy that music enthusiasts still appreciate and cherish. And besides... radio is always free!

CHAPTER 9

Here, There and Everywhere!
The Bands and Venues outside of Detroit

"...it helps that in Michigan everyone goes inside from November through April."
Author Charles Baxter|

Anyone who has ever picked up a guitar or a pair of drum sticks knows the feeling. In thousands of garages and basements across Michigan, they sweated over the hits of the day. The author has a theory that the reason Michigan bands are so good is the long, cold winters, where jamming in basements and at parties is the best way to pass the time while improving their chops.

But despite what some might think, Detroit was not the center of the rock-n-roll universe, and almost overnight, by the late 1960s as the teen clubs faded other concert venues popped up and bands from the Upper Peninsula to

the Indiana state line jammed. Here are just a few of the popular bands that were not from Motor City.

• The Amboy Dukes: hailing from Grand Rapids, The Amboy Dukes, led by Ted Nugent, achieved success with their fierce and energetic rock music.

• The MC5: Although they are often associated with Detroit, the MC5 actually formed in Lincoln Park, a suburb of Detroit. Their politically charged rock music had a significant impact on the counterculture scene.

• The Bossmen from Flint, Michigan, formed in 1964 and gained popularity with their blend of rock and R&B music. The band was fronted by Dick Wagner, who later became a renowned guitarist and songwriter, working with artists like Alice Cooper and Lou Reed.

- The Frost: Originally from Alpena, The Frost gained popularity in the late 1960s with their psychedelic and hard rock sound. Their song 'Rock and Roll Music' became an anthem of the times.

These are just a few examples of Michigan bands from the 1960s that were not from or based in Detroit. There were many other talented groups across the state during that time, each contributing to the rich musical landscape of Michigan. While these bands didn't achieve national success, they were stars of the mitten, playing everywhere from Teen Center Dances to School Sock Hops to bars, special events and popular concert halls like The Grande, The Eastown and the Vaniety Ballroom. But its important to understand that this was a phenomena that was not exclusive to the big city of Detroit but was occurring in the small towns across the state affecting youth organizations everywhere and providing a vital place for youth to congregate.

'Tonto and the Renegades'
Grand Ledge, MI 1964-1969

Uncle Russ Goes South
The Cleveland Grande?

At first glance, late-Sixties Cleveland and Detroit were very similar. Before imports, the steel and auto industries put a heavy ethnic population firmly into the middle class. Similar housing, politics and oh, those nasty winters, but it bred a community with strong opinions and convictions on a wide range of topics and rock music was one of them. Both had a lot of home-grown talent and with audiences demanding the best the top acts traveled back and forth uniting the cities in a rock bond.

CKLW-AM boomed over the airwaves giving its neighbors across Lake Erie a generous sample of Motor City music, while the 50,000 watt blowtorch KYW-AM, later changing its calls to WKYC-AM, returned the favor across dozens of states. Motown Records' Berry Gordy was quoted saying Cleveland was a convenient stopping point for Detroit acts because the city had a rich musical heritage and folks with a keen ear for entertainment. He'd bring his up-and-coming stars to the city's 'Leo's Casino night club' to introduce them in another town because their friends and neighbors would be cheering them on back home. If they clicked in Cleveland, it was a

major first step. If they didn't measure up they returned for more work and rehearsal back up north.

Like Detroit, the Cleveland area had plenty of teen dance clubs as well as show bars to see emerging and established talent and, of course, theaters and concert halls, but the Motor City had a huge advantage in one key area. It had the Grande Ballroom. Russ Gibb saw the potential for a mid-sized venue and in 1968 he made his move. He found the right sized theater in the old WHK Auditorium, a decaying old vaudeville house fifteen minutes from downtown that was in the same building as the AM radio station and its new FM format on WMMS-FM. Keep in mind that this was before local Belkin Productions became one of the most respected concert promoters in the country, and some smaller operations were booking acts like Big Brother and the Holding Company, Velvet Underground, Traffic and Pacific Gas and Electric along with dozens of name folk acts at La Cave, a small club near the city's University Circle. Gibbs had an established name and connections, Those were also the days when live music could be heard every night of the week at dozens of clubs in both cities featuring skilled musical acts getting better with every note and performance. It was a great opportunity to show each city what the other had to offer in support of national acts on the verge of stardom.

It was time to expand the Gibb empire and after checking out a number of Cleveland venues he settled on the old WHK Auditorium. Years before when the radio station moved in it claimed naming rights, though it rarely used the theater. A paying tenant was more than welcome! Opening night was October 25, 1968, and a small blurb in the Plain Dealer News entertainment section stated, "The first 2000 get in free!" for a Thursday night show with Quicksilver Messenger Service, The Case of E.T. Hooley and The James Gang with guitarist Joe Walsh.

There's no doubt Grande Cleveland was still getting name acts despite the bare bones stage and auditorium. Bookings included Blood Sweat and Tears, Jeff Beck, Procol Harum, and Rotary Connection among others, with plenty of Detroit and Cleveland acts in the mix. There was also an definable odor and an off-color patina on the molding that essentially said, "old….but cool!

The theater wasn't used on a regular basis for many years. WHK and WMMS moved out in 1976 and it briefly opened as the "New Hipp" showing films but couldn't draw any crowds. Finally, another noted concert promoter, Hank LoConti re-opened his Agora Club at that location in 1986 hosting a wide variety of bands including David Bowie, Crosby Stills and Nash and a list of names that would make Russ Gibb proud. After a serious renovation the Agora is still thriving today.

The band 'The Case of E.T. Hooley' played both the Detroit and 'Grande South' venues, including opening night in Cleveland. Singer Chip Fitzgerald had memories of the Euclid Avenue stage, saying, "It was a fascinating old building with spooky areas upstairs", though the Detroit ballroom seemed bigger. They'd opened for Buddy Guy on one of their frequent trips to Michigan and got to know folks in the MC5 and other bands to get a good idea what audiences at both locations expected. Fitzgerald says, "Playing the Grande immediately put you in the 'Big Boys' club and opened many doors to larger venues. It was great to have this endorsement on your resume. You always did your best to bring your 'A Game' because there were always agents, club owners in the audience. Once you won the fans… they loved you!"

Russ Gibb and Grande Cleveland were usually open to giving bands an opportunity to play even if they were still doing covers. Hempstead Incident was one of them and, as bass player Dale Robeson recalls, "Barry Weingart, our manager, got in touch with the band just hours before showtime to inform us about the gig (opening for Procol Harum) and logistically it was a nightmare!," he said. "Two members lived in the eastern suburbs of Cleveland… Donny Better in Cleveland Heights and our new keyboard player Bruce 'Biff" Feller, in Gates Mills. The remaining members were all living in Lorain County on the far west side. Our drummer Carl, in Elyria , singer John Fergusons was in Lorain, and I was in Avon Lake," he said. "Plus, all the equipment was in Gates Mills where we practiced (in the carriage house on the estate of Cleveland Indians great Bob Feller. Biff was Bob's youngest, and least favored son.). I don't remember how, but we did manage to get everybody and the equipment down to the Grande and get set up with minutes to spare."

Like other bands, getting booked at the Grande was inspiring, but you had a lot to prove. Job number one? Give 'em a show! Robeson explains, "Playing on a real stage was really exciting, and I was very grateful the stage lights prevented me from seeing the size of the audience. The crowd was kind to us

considering we were just a cover band....but regardless a very tight cover band."

People still have fond memories of the Cleveland Grande. Local art studio Raw Sugar Studios pays tribute to some of the venue's most memorable shows with a series of commemorative posters that, frankly, should have been issued when it was worth risking your safety for a memorable moment in your personal musical history. Ending in 1969 the Cleveland Grande was a brief shining star in both local and international Rock-n-Roll!

- *Mike Olszewski*

CHAPTER 10

The Influencers
Power to the People

*"I aimed at the public's heart,
and by accident I hit it in the stomach!"*
John Sinclair, Rainbow People's Party

They say that a single person can't really affect change yet throughout history it is the only thing that has. That the 1960s in the Motor City was special goes without saying from the music of Motown to the 1968 World Series Championship Tigers. There were a few individuals who where at the forefront of Detroit rock-n-roll, the counter culture and the youth movement of the mitten. Here's just a few who helped usher in change.

Russ Gibb
1931 - 2019
Promoter, Radio DJ, High School Teacher
Perhaps more than any other counter culture figure of the 1960s Uncle Russ was first among equals. He was a true Machiavellian creator with fingers in all sorts of pies from The Grande to his radio show he led the way and it was

always all about others and the kids. In edition to owning the Grande Ballroom he is perhaps best known for his role in the "Paul is Dead" phenomenon. He retired in 2004, having spent 42 years teaching in the Dearborn public school system. For 16 years, he produced the student-run cable TV show 'Back Porch Video'. Gibb also owned and leased several other live music venues around the Midwest including The Eastown, Michigan Theater, Birmingham Palladium and the Cleveland Grande. He invested in the rock magazine CREEM in 1969. In 1970 Gibb helped produce the Goose Lake Music Festival which attracted a crowd of 200,000 people to mid-Michigan. In the 70s he brought cable licenses which he sold in the 1980s becoming a millionaire. More than any other person he helped establish a thriving counter culture community in Michigan and the mid-west.

John Sinclair
Activist, Writer, Poet, Band Manager, Event Producer, Founder, White Panther/ Rainbow People's Party, Pro Agitator

Busted for 2 joints and put in State Prison it was clear the establishment wanted to make an example out of

Sinclair. He had been very outspoken against the war and also had not been silent about the brutality of the Detroit Police Department. He was involved in the underground newspaper 'The 5th Estate'. He was the poster man for local the anti-war movement. Currently he's an award winning author and poet living in an undisclosed location somewhere on the planet earth.

Sinclair Milestones
- President, Trans-Love Energies, Inc.
- Manager/Producer The MC-5
- Manager, Mitch Ryder, The Rockets, Guardian Angel
- Editor & Publisher, Ann Arbor Sun newspaper
- Founder & Talent Mgr., Free Concerts in the Parks
- Author, Guitar Army: Street Writings/Prison Writings
- Founder & Talent Mgr, People's Ballroom, Ann Arbor
- Editor-In-Chief, Detroit Sun Newspaper
- Adjunct Prof., Music History, Wayne State University
- Chairman, Rainbow Peoples Party, Ann Arbor

Ed 'Punch' Andrews
Band Manager, Booker, Record Producer, Musician
Involved with mega-bands Grand Funk Rail Road and Bob Seger, Andrews was a top band booker in Detroit as well as being a musician and award winning record producer. Andrews opened his fourth Hideout teen club at the end of 1966. He produced Bob Seger and The Silver Bullet Band and also served as the band's Manager for more than 35 years. He also managed Kid Rock. He almost single handedly made Grand Funk a household name and from a local band to international stardom for

the boys from Flint. He retired in 2007 and is rumored to be working on a book about his time in Detroit.

Barry Kramer
Publisher of CREEM Magazine, Record Store owner
Kramer, who owned record stores and head shops in Detroit decided to invest in a publication called CREEM one of his employees had started. He had a talent for spotting talent and the Magazine and its real roots began in 1969. The staff had a love-hate relationship with the publisher over the years. Depending on who ya talk to Kramer, age 37, tragically either committed suicide or accidentally died by nitrous oxide suffocation in 1981.

Robin Seymour
1928 - 2020
DJ, TV Host, Promoter
A radio personality at CKLW and WKMH Seymour was also the host of the popular television series' 'Teen Town' and 'Swingin' Time' in Detroit on WWJ-TV. He started in radio as a child actor on the Lone Ranger Show and

eventually became one of the country's longest-serving DJs. He pioneered rock-n-roll on the Detroit airwaves and his shows were road maps for Dick's American Bandstand. He also introduced artists and was one of the first to play black artists to white listeners such as Stevie Wonder, The Four Tops, Martha and the Vandellas, and The Supremes. After the 1967 riots Seymour launched beautification projects around Detroit with a huge kickoff concert at Cobo Arena. He semi-retired in 1980 and move out of Michigan.

Dave Leone
1942-1999
Diversified Management Agency, Hideout Records and Hideout Night Clubs

Detroit-born Dave Leone was a man who had varied interests; booker, promoter, nightclub owner, record label exec, producer and songwriter. For more than 40 years from 1969 to 1987 he was the go-to guy for booking top quality Rock-n-Roll talent at DMA (Diversified Management Agency). Both local and national bands were booked. He started off as a prolific club owner creating the legendary Hideout Clubs with Punch Andrews. The very first Hideout Club was at Harper

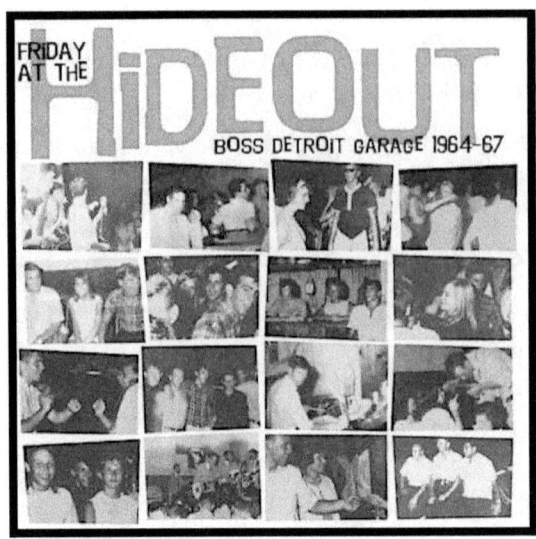

Blvd. and Lennon St. in Harper Woods but by the time it was all over in the early to mid 70s there were 7 of them over the years providing a vital place for both teens and the bands they loved, to rock.

With Hideout Records, Leone, nicknamed 'Papa Leone' recorded the who's who of Detroit Rock from Bob Seger to the Pleasure Seekers and from Ted Nugent to the Underdogs and the late Glenn Frey to name but a few. Dave Leone passed away in 1999 of a heart attack, he was the author's neighbor in Farmington Hills and the Author was on the DMA roster of artists in the late 1970's.

Hugh "Jeep" Holland
1947 - 1998
Record Producer, Talent Booker, Event Planner
"Jeep" Holland, a University of Michigan student was captivated by the mid-'1960s rock music explosion. While running Discount Records on State Street, he threw himself into the local scene as an agent (A2 Productions), Manager, Producer and supporter of area bands and musicians, including the SRC, The Rationals.

He founded A-Square Records to promote his bands and the local music scene in general. The storied music lineups at Detroit's venues were overseen by Jeep. He also created the famed 'Free Concerts in the Park' program which hosted free rock concerts on Sunday in parks in and around Ann Arbor.

Gary Grimshaw
1946 – 2014
Artist, Activist

An American graphic artist active in Detroit and San Francisco who specialized in designing rock concert posters, Grimshaw was also a radical political activist with the White Panther Party and related organizations. The Grande Ballroom in Detroit, famous for its role in the countercultural music scene of the 1960s, had a number of talented artists who designed its posters.

The most notable artist associated with the Grande Ballroom posters is Gary Grimshaw. He was the primary designer for the venue and created iconic psychedelic concert posters featuring vibrant colors, intricate lettering, and surreal imagery. His unique style perfectly captured the psychedelic rock spirit of the time and helped establish the visual language for that era.

Other artists who contributed to the Grande concert posters include Carl Lundgren, who designed notable

posters for bands like The Who and Cream, and Dennis Loren, who was known for his intricate designs. The Grande Ballroom posters, with their visually stunning artwork, became collectibles and symbols of the counterculture movement. They not only advertised upcoming shows but also captured the essence of the music and cultural revolution taking place in Detroit during the 1960s. The posters are highly sought after today, appreciated not only for their historical significance but also for their artistic value.

Other Influencers

Detroit in the 1960s, had a number of influential band managers and concert promoters who tho lesser known still played pivotal roles in nurturing the city's music scene and supporting local talent. Here are a few more notable figures from that era:

•**Mike Quatro:** A notable band manager and promoter who worked with various Detroit-based acts, including Bob Seger, Alice Cooper, and Suzi Quatro. He was instrumental in launching the careers of these artists and guiding them to national and international recognition.

•**The Detroit Artists Workshop**: The Detroit Artists Workshop, founded by John Sinclair, played a significant role in supporting local musicians and promoting their work. This collective provided a creative platform for artists to collaborate, perform, and experiment with different artistic forms, contributing to Detroit music.

•**The Grand Parlor**: Managed by Robin Seymour, the Grande Parlor was an important venue and musician collective in Detroit during the mid to late 1960s. It hosted performances by local and national acts, and Seymour's involvement significantly influenced the music scene in the city.

•**The Hideout Clubs**: The Hideout, managed by Mike Clark, was another influential venue in the Detroit music scene. It served as a hub for local rock bands, hosting performances and promoting new talent. The Hideout became a gathering place for musicians and fans alike.

These band managers and concert promoters, were essential in supporting and promoting Detroit's music scene. They provided opportunities for local artists, organized concerts and events, and helped establish Detroit as a vibrant and influential music city. Their contributions continue to be recognized and celebrated in the city's musical history.

Perhaps more than any other publication, person or place it was CREEM Magazine that helped to solidify Detroit's rep as the city of Rock-n-Roll and it was Boy Howdy that introduced us! Here, for the first time, is how our favorite mascot came to be.

CHAPTER 11

The Boy Howdy Story
How CREEM's Mascot Came to Be a Rock-n-Rock Icon

Boy Howdy – eh?? You've seen the t-shirts…

Robert Crumb looked just like his images, as reflected in the popular underground press at the time… skinny, disheveled, unkempt…peering over little round glasses. He was, in fact, so nondescript that he immediately recognizable. He came up to the counter and said, "I hear that you're starting a magazine…". It wasn't really a question.. and so I just said, "Yeah".

The first issue of the magazine was still a coupla weeks away… according to the Editor but a Crumb art piece would help enormously in terms of streetcred (although, in them days, there was no such word as streetcred!)

"Would you like a cover for it?" he asked, politely. He didn't seem at all pushy.. at all aware of his real value to a project like ours… although I'm sure that he realized that the Janis cover and Zap Comix empire alone would add enormous value to anything he presented afterwards. The Editor asked him what he would charge for a cover and kinda hemmed and hawed a little and then said, "Fifty bucks".

The Editor knew that he would have to get permission from the publisher to pay that much – after all, the magazine's artists weren't getting paid anything at all, so far. Asked if he could take any less Crumb said, in hushed tones, "No – I need the fifty to get a clap shot… and rather quickly!"

"But how long will it take to come up with the cover," the Editor asked. "I can have it to ya tomorrow" he said quietly. The Editor swallowed hard and said "Sure – go ahead" and then Crumb left. Later that day, the publisher came to take the takings and he was told what had been done... He started shouting – not an unusual situation. It was explained to him that it was the one and only R. CRUMB and we would get a cover and that it surenuff would be worth fifty bucks. "Give him thirty!" he yelled. It was explained to him why that wouldn't work... after all, the boy had NEEDS, doncha know... but he kept on yelling "thirty bucks – no more!" as he left in a huff.

Stature of R. Crumb in Dartmouth, UK

The next morning Crumb was there as the Editor unlocked the door. He showed off the artwork and it became the cover for issue 2. They were off and runnin! Later R Crumb was commissioned to create our favorite mascot and the rest is history.

♪

Sock Hops Enliven Weekends

Providing excellent entertainment for the lively crowds who frequent the various sock hops, the Scot Richard Case renders a unique interpretation of a popular song.

WALLY and The NEW MASTERTONES
LINCOLN PARK J.C SPONSORED
1st PLACE "BATTLE of THE BANDS" WINNER 1968

Formerly Seen On:
T.V. SWINGING TIME - T.V CLUB 1270
RADIO W.K.N.R - BOB GREEN - THE JOE VAN SHOW

Appeared With and Friends of:
THE BEATLES - HERMAN'S HERMITS - THE MONKIES
THE ROLLING STONES - THE BYRDS - THE SUPREMES & OTHERS

WILL APPEAR "IN PERSON"

PLACE SOUTHGATE REC. CENTER   SAT: JUNE 29
DATE   SAT: JUNE   TIME 7-?

Personal Manager
MR. JIM BEE
2027 Buckingham
Lincoln Park, Mich.
388-1164

CHAPTER 12
Pictures & Clips

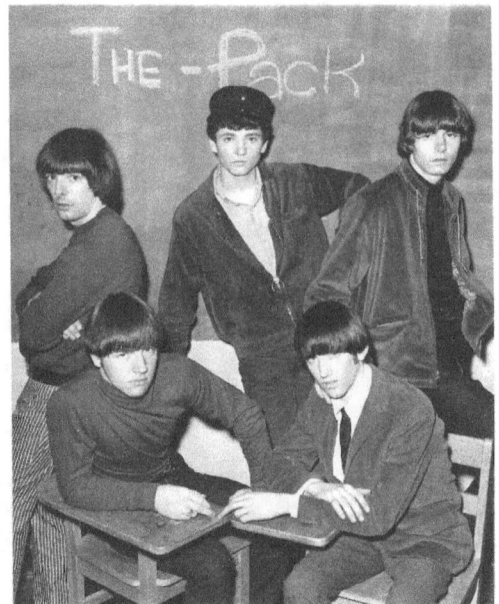

to myself, "Kids in England have got no manners anymore,'" he says.

know who had a drinking problem at 15," continues Herman. "By 18 I was a man . . . be

Detroit's top tunes

'Honky Tonk Women'
'Give Peace a Chance'

1.	"Honky Tonk Women"	Rolling Stones
2.	"In the Year 2525"	Zager and Evans
3.	"Crystal Blue Persuasion"	Tommy James
4.	"A Boy Named Sue"	Johnny Cash
5.	"Sweet Caroline"	Neil Diamond
6.	"Sugar, Sugar"	The Archies
7.	"Soul Deep"	Box Tops
8.	"Give Peace a Chance"	Plastic Ono Band
9.	"Lay Lady Lay"	Bob Dylan
10.	"Laughing"	Guess Who

ROCK it to me!

BY ICE ALEXANDER

Who really owns the Wilson Mower Pursuit—or who really owns John Levy? Or who really owns Dick Sloss? Points to ponder.

... How come the Frost didn't have contracts for most of their West Coast gigs? Or how come their road managers spent a full day at an airport?

... The Moody Blues sent us another of their letters saying they wouldn't be able to come and play. We are opening an exhibition of Moody Blues letters as they are classic examples of contract escapers. Like those letters you used to write to your school when you wanted a day off—the ones that ran, "I won't be at school today 'coz I'm sick and our phone is cut off so you can't call."

... THE SUNDAY Funnies have stopped singing and taken up a strong act which includes microphone building and tearing P.A.'s in half.

... The Sky's bass player looks like Scott Morgan with braces or, nearer the truth, braces with Scott Morgan.

... Ten Years After were here again—just in case anybody who saw them thought it was just a film of their last two Grande appearances.

... Chip Stevens Blues Band is, surprisingly, very, very fine.

... Ever notice that you never see the Sun's lead player and the Third Power's drummer together.

... PAT YOUNG finally bought an album!

... Speaking of albums — how incredible is the new Three Dogs Night album—it's really so much more exciting and intricate than their first.

... If John Lennon is as broke as he says he is he should choose cheaper hotels to spend whole weeks in. And if Brian Wilson is as broke as he says he is why doesn't his writing revert to the caliber it was at the time of "God Only Knows!"

... I don't care what anyone says, I think Dionne Warwick's new single is one of the best things I have heard in years.

... Thank you, Roy Feldman for playing music!

... THE GRAND Funk Railroad single, at first, sounded like Jeff Beck—now it sounds like the Grand Funk Railroad.

... It seems strange to see Pentangle on Robin Seymour's TV show on Channel 62. I don't know why but it does!

... Bill Figg plays vibes on the Rational's album which, so far, is going very well.

... Russ Gibb earns most of his money playing for the Brownsville Station. (Cubby Gibb?)

... The Savage Grace must be making a lot of money as Jerry now has two phones—so does Jeep but he only knows one of the numbers.

... WJKB AM is becoming pretty heavy although the station's policy has generally been rather blasé, suddenly it seems that the DJs are being allowed more freedom to air their social and political views and they're using it well.

... What is the connection between Al Kooper and the Johnny Winter bust? More points to ponder!

... If you can think of anything else that should be said then say it.

THE FROST
Where were their contracts?

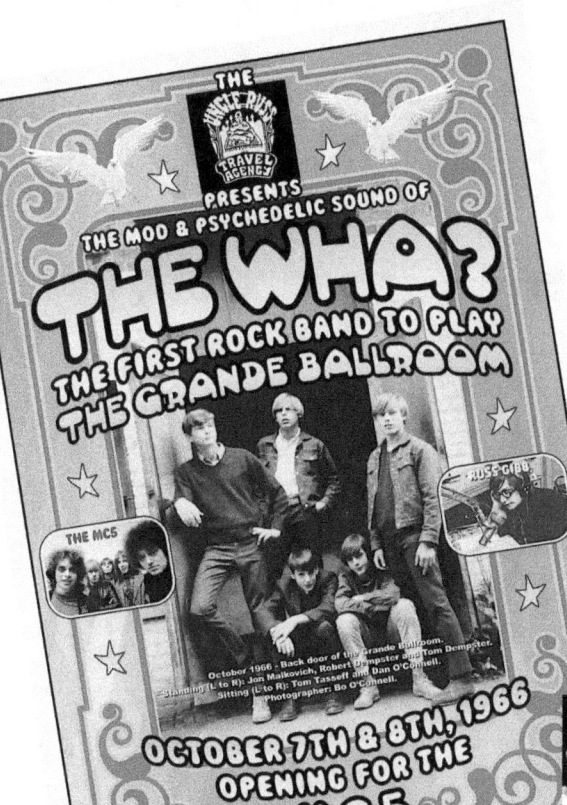

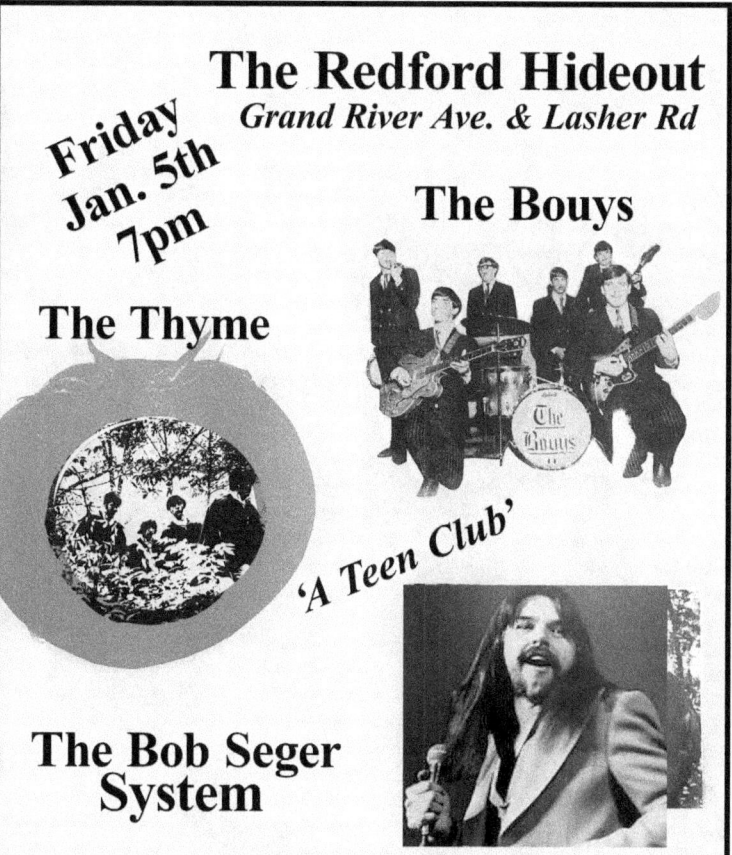

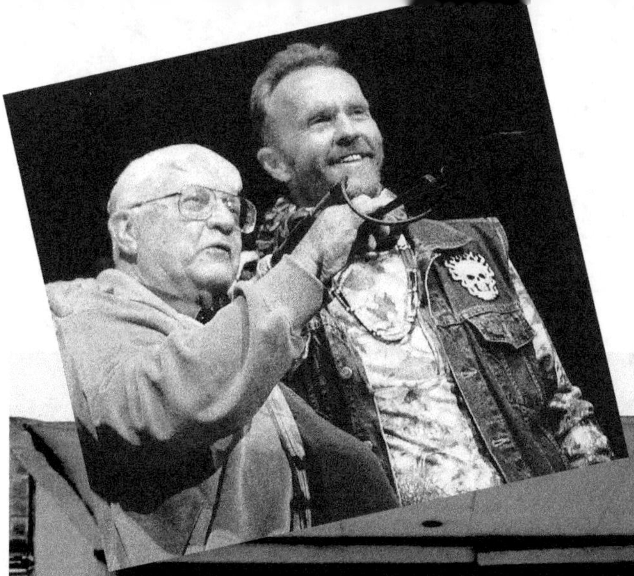

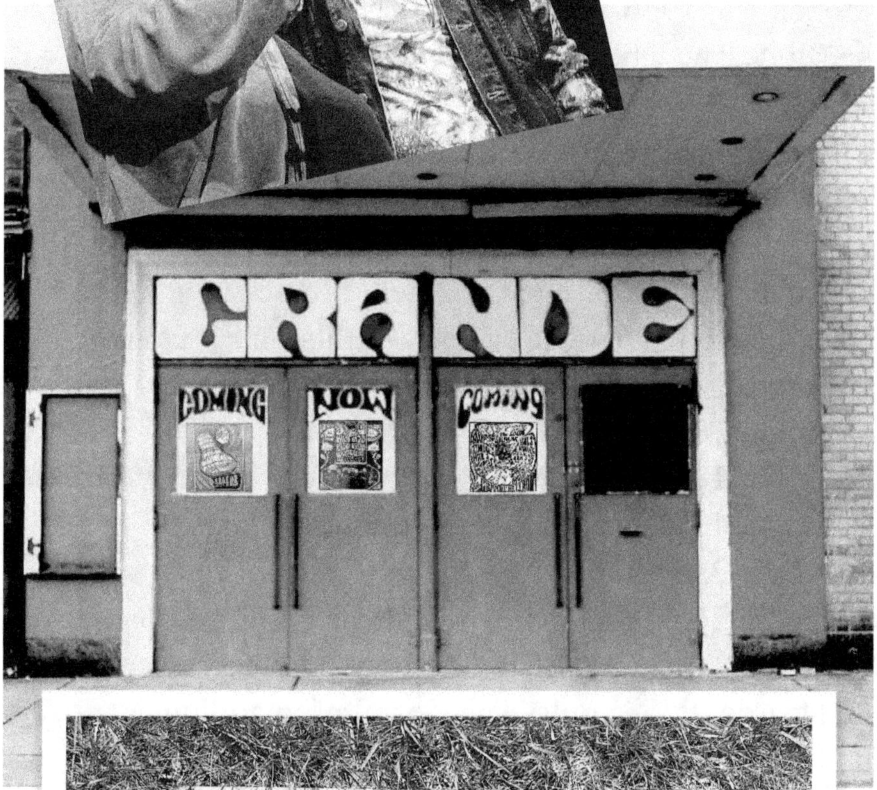
GRANDE
COMING
NOW
COMING

RUSSELL J. GIBB
JUNE 15, 1931 – APRIL 30, 2019
BELOVED SON, FRIEND & TEACHER
DETROIT ROCK AND ROLL VISIONARY & PROMOTER

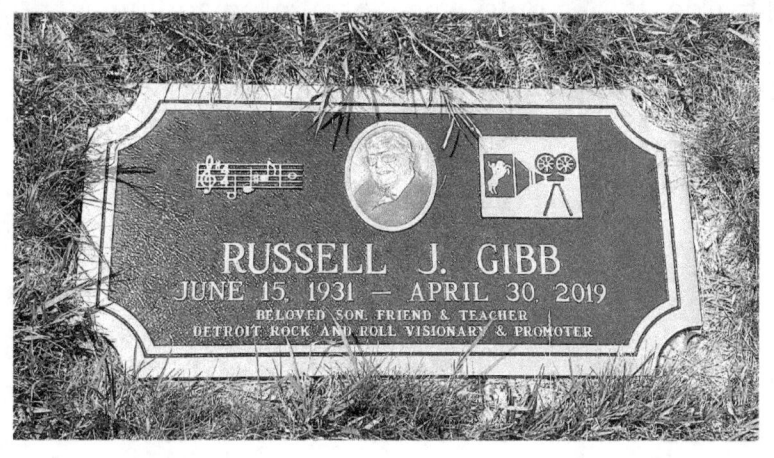

GRANDE BALLROOM
Concert List

1966
October 7-8, 1966 – - GRAND OPENING!
The MC5, The Chosen Few, The Wha?
October 14-15, 1966 – MC5, Woolies, Freeway
October 21-22, 1966 – MC5, The Prime Movers
October 28, 1966 – MC5,The Southbound Freeway
October 29, 1966 – Southbound Freeway, The Chosen Few
November 4, 1966 – The Bossmen, Freeway
November 5, 1966 – MC5, The Southbound Freeway
November 11, 1966 – The Hitch-Hikers, Freeway
November 12, 1966 – MC5, The Thyme
November 18, 1966 – Walking Wounded, Wha?, Poor Souls
November 19, 1966 – MC5 & "Mystery Bands"
November 25, 1966 – The Jagged Edge, MC5
November 26, 1966 – MC5, The Black & Blues Band
December 2-3, 1966 – The Southbound Freeway,
The Hearde, Poor Souls, The Cosmic Expanding,
The Psychedelic Flipout
December 9, 1966 – The Jagged Edge, Ourselves
December 10, 1966 – MC5, The Kynde
December 16, 1966 – The Landeers, The Plague
December 17, 1966 – MC5, The Wha?
Dec. 22-23, 1966 - MC5, Green Grass, Suburban Roots
Dec. 26, 1966 – "The 5th Estate 1st Annual Freak Out".
MC5, The Cosmic Expanding Blues Band
December 29, 1966 – MC5, The Black & Blues Band
December 30, 1966 – The Taboos, The Thyme
Dec. 31, 1966 – MC5, Cosmic Blues Band, Poor Souls

1967

January 6, 1967 – The Walking Wounded
January 7, 1967 – MC5, Seventh Seal
January 13, 1967 – Southbound Freeway, Unrelated Segments
January 14, 1967 – MC5, The Cosmic Expanding Blues Band
January 20, 1967 – MC5, The Trees
January 21, 1967 – SRC, The Passing Clouds
January 27, 1967 – The Plague, C-Water Blues
January 28, 1967 – MC5, The Vernor Highway Blues Band
January 29, 1967 – CANCELLED due to Sinclair & Co. drug bust!
February 3, 1967 – The Wha?, Poor Souls, Brand X
February 4, 1967 – MC5, The Raven, The Harvard Street Blues
February 10, 1967 – The Thyme, People
February 11, 1967 – The Rationals, The Zymodics, The Wha?
February 17, 1967 – The Barons, The Ashmollyan Quintet
February 18, 1967 – The Landeers, The Cosmic Blues Band
February 24, 1967 – Scot Richard Case, The Village Beaus
February 25, 1967 – The Jagged Edge, The D.S.R.
March 3, 1967 – Ourselves, The Zymodics
March 4, 1967 – MC5, The Apostles, The Belshires
March 10, 1967 – We Who Are, Poor Souls
March 11, 1967 – Southbound Freeway, The Frut, Passing Clouds
March 17, 1967 – MC5, Sixth Street
March 18, 1967 – Scot Richard Case, The Strange Fate, Gang
March 24, 1967 – The Landeers, The Henchmen
March 25, 1967 – MC5, City Limits
March 30, 1967 – Scot Richard Case, Somethin' Else
March 31, 1967 – The Thyme, Wild Cargo, Yesterday's Shadows
April 1, 1967 – Detroit Blues Ball, The Jagged Edge, Seventh Seal, The Back & Back Boo Funny Music Band
April 2, 1967 – Benefit for Senator Roger Craig. MC5, Billy C. & The Sunshine, Seventh Seal, C-Water Blues

April 7-8, 1967 – The Rationals, Restless Set, The
April 14, 1967 – The Weeds, Changing Times
April 15, 1967 – One Way Street, The Thyme, Gang
April 21, 1967 – The Jagged Edge, Sons of Sound
April 22, 1967 – Scot Richard Case, Manchild, The New Spirit
April 23, 1967 – Benefit for the Warren/Forest Sun.
 MC5, Billy C. & The Sunshine.
April 28, 1967 – The Jagged Edge, The Trees, The Wild Woodies

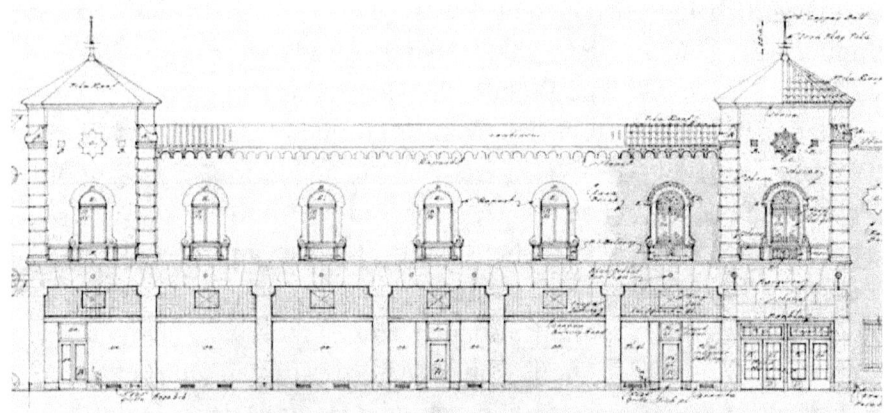

April 29, 1967 – The Metrics, The Strange Fate, Buckingham 5
May 5, 1967 – Billy C. & The Sunshine, The Primates
May 6, 1967 – The Wha?, The Strange Fate, Harmond St Blues
May 12, 1967 – Ourselves, The Berry Patch, The Hearde
May 13, 1967 – The Apostles, Echoes from a Broken Mirror
May 19, 1967 – Scot Richard Case, December's Children
May 20, 1967 – The Thyme, Odds & Ends
May 26, 1967 – The Southbound Freeway, Cowardly Thangs
May 27, 1967 – Harmond Street Blues, Vernor Highway Band
June 2, 1967 – The Rationals, C-Water Blues
June 3, 1967 – The Jagged Edge, The Belshires
June 9, 1967 – The Apostles, The Morticians
June 10, 1967 – The Thyme, The Eccentrics
June 16, 1967 – The Jagged Edge, Shifting Sands

June 17, 1967 – MC5, Those Guys
June 20, 1967 – "Love Prom"
Spike Drivers, Jazz Disciples, The Group
June 23, 1967 – MC5, The Phogg
June 24, 1967 – Scot Richard Case, The Up-Set
June 30, 1967 – Echoes, Broken Mirror, The Southampton Rowe
July 1, 1967 – MC5, The English Ryders
July 7, 1967 – The Thyme, The Hideaways, The Malibus
July 8, 1967 – Ourselves, The Berry Patch
July 14, 1967 – The Rationals, The Bump
July 15, 1967 – Jagged Edge, Craig Sutherland Movement
July 21-22, 1967 – Tim Buckley, MC5, The Shaggs, Up!
July 28, 1967 – Scot Richard Case, The Euphonic Aggregation
July 29, 1967 – The Apostles, The Up-Set
August 4, 1967 – The Thyme, Odds & Ends
August 5, 1967 – The Apostles, The Bouys
August 11-12, 1967 – The Grateful Dead, The Rationals, The Southbound Freeway, The Bishops, The Ashmollyan Quintet
August 18, 1967 – The Thyme, The Uncalled Four
August 19, 1967 – The Shaggs, The Troyes
August 25, 1967 – The Thyme, The Apostles, Mother's Children
August 26, 1967 – Scot Richard Case, MC5, Certified Chalk
August 27, 1967 – Benefit for Trans Love Energies, MC5, The Spike Drivers, Billy C. & The Sunshine
September 1-2, 1967 – The Chambers Brothers, MC-5, Thyme
September 8, 1967 – Scot Richard Case, The Bouys
September 9, 1967 – The Rationals, The Jagged Edge, The Up
September 15, 1967 – MC5, Gang, Ourselves
September 16, 1967 – The Pack, Odds & Ends, Ashmollyan
September 22, 1967 – The Southbound Freeway, Our Mother's Children, Billy C. & The Sunshine
September 23, 1967 – MC5, The Bouys, The F.D.A.
September 24, 1967 – Benefit for the Warren Forest-Sun. MC5, The Up, The Charles Moore Ensemble.

September 29, 1967 – The Apostles, Eastside Orphans, Happiness
September 30, 1967 – MC5, The Spike Drivers
October 1, 1967 – "DEVA Presents", The F.D.A, MC5, Gang, The Heard, Period, The Rationals, The Thyme, Ourselves, Our Mother's Children, Poor Souls
October 6, 1967 – Scot Richard Case, Billy C. & The Sunshine
October 7, 1967 – MC5, Gang, Odds & Ends
October 13-15, 1967 – Cream, MC5, Thyme, Rationals, Apostles
October 20, 1967 – The Pack, Gold, Our Mother's Children
October 21, 1967 – MC5, Gang, Billy C. & The Sunshine
October 27, 1967 – MC5, The Rationals, The Prime Movers
October 28, 1967 – The James Gang, Up, Avery Assemblage
October 29, 1967 – Trans Love Benefit. MC-5, Gold.
November 3-5, 1967 – The Paupers, Gang, The Thyme, The Up, The Rationals, MC5, The Apostles, Peter Max
November 10-11, 1967 – The James Cotton Blues Band, MC5, The Thyme, 11th Billy C. & The Sunshine, The Apostles
November 17, 1967 –SRC, The Apostles, The Lost Generation
November 18, 1967 – Odds & Ends, Mother's Child, Epidemic
November 23, 1967 – MC5, Scot Richard Case
November 24-25, 1967 – The Fugs, 24th Gang, The Ashmollyan Quintet, MC5
November 26, 1967 – Benefit for John Sinclair Defense Fund. The Fugs, MC5, Billy C. & The Sunshine
December 1-2, 1967 – The Chambers Brothers, Children, The Thyme, The Up
December 8-9, 1967 – Moby Grape, The Rationals, The Wilson Mower Pursuit, MC5
December 15-17, 1967 – The Vanilla Fudge, The Thyme, The Rationals, Our Mother's Children, The Epidemic, MC5
December 21, 1967 – The Paul Butterfield Blues Band, The Thyme, The Rationals or The Apostles
December 22-23, 1967 – Cream, MC5, The Sunshine, Soap
December 25, 1967 – MC5, The Rationals, The Up, Odds & Ends

December 26-27, 1967 – The Lyman Woodard Trio, Billy C. and The Sunshine, The Talismen, MC5, The Up
December 28, 1967 – The Woolies, Soap, Heavy Metal Kids
December 29-30, 1967 – John Lee Hooker, The Apostles, The Pack, The Gang
December 31, 1967 – MC5, Billy C. & The Sunshine, Prime Movers & The Apostles

1968
January 5-6, 1968 – Clear Light, Gipsy Blue, Children
January 12-13, 1968 – The Buddy Guy Blues Band, The Gang,
January 19-20, 1968 – Scot Richard Case, Apple Pie Motherhood, The Amboy Dukes, The Psychedelic Stooges
January 23, 1968 – John Mayall's Bluesbreakers, The Rationals, Odds & Ends

January 26-27, 1968 – The Lyman Woodard Trio, The Thyme, The Rationals, The Jagged Edge
February 2-3, 1968 – Beacon Street Union, MC5, Charging Rhinoceros of Soul
February 9, 1968 – The Frost, Children
February 10, 1968 – The Jagged Edge, The Ashmollyan Quintet
February 16-17, 1968 – Canned Heat, Thyme, Carousel, The Up
February 18, 1968 – The Byrds, Rationals, Wilson Mower Pursuit
February 23, 1968 – The Frut of the Loom, Tiers
February 24, 1968 – SRC, Born Blues, The Grass Route
March 1-2, 1968 – Big Brother & The Holding Company, MC5, Pink Peech Mob, Tiffany Shade & Family Dump Truck
March 3, 1968 – Blood, Sweat & Tears, Carousel, The Psychedelic Stooges
March 8, 1968 – The Electric Prunes, The Thyme
March 9, 1968 – The Who, Soap, The Schillings
March 10, 1968 – The Electric Prunes unconfirmed
March 15-16, 1968 – The Youngbloods, The Rationals, The Up & The James Gang
March 17, 1968 – MC5, The Thyme
March 23, 1968 – "The Grande Scene at the State Fair Coliseum". Eric Burdon & the Animals, The Grateful Dead, Air Apparent, The Apostles, The Jagged Edge. Moved from the Michigan State Fairgrounds Coliseum
March 24, 1968 – "Tribal Stomp" MC5, The Up, Pink Peech Mob, Odds & Ends, Gold, The Psychedelic Stooges
March 29-31, 1968 – The Fugs, Sly & The Family Stone, MC5, The Psychedelic Stooges
April 5-6, 1968 – The Troggs, The Apostles, Tiffany Shade, MC5
April 7, 1968 – Junior Wells, The Psychedelic Stooges, The Up
April 10, 1968 – The Mothers of Invention
April 12-13, 1968 – Traffic, The Jagged Edge, The Ashmollyan Quintet, Panic & The Pack
April 14, 1968 – The Thyme & "Other Goodies"

April 17, 1968 – MC5, The Jagged Edge, Psychedelic Stooges
April 18, 1968 – Scot Richard Case, The Thyme, The Ashmollyan
April 19-21, 1968 – Cream postponed until June, Children & Poor Richard's Almanac, The Rationals, The Frost, James Gang, The Psychedelic Stooges
April 26, 1968 – The Rationals, The Thyme, Apple Corps
April 27, 1968 – The Jagged Edge, The Thyme, Orange Fuzz
April 28, 1968 – The Mothers of Invention, The Psychedelic Stooges, Charging Rhinoceros of Soul, Late Show MC5, Carousel
May 3-4, 1968 – The Yardbirds, The Frost, The Stuart Avery Assemblage, MC5, Odds & Ends
May 5, 1968 – "Surprise Goodies"
May 10-11, 1968 – James Cotton Blues Band, MC5, Buffey Reed Phenomena, The Up
May 12, 1968 – Children, East Side Orphans
May 17-18, 1968 – Procol Harum, Influence, Nirvana, Nickel Plate
May 19, 1968 – The Soul Remains, Muff
May 24-26, 1968 – The Paul Butterfield Blues Band, The Frost, Buffy Reed Phenomena, 25th The Jagged Edge, Fox, MC5, The Psychedelic Stooges
May 29-30, 1968 – The Crazy World of Arthur Brown, Toad, Carousel, The Jagged Edge, Charging Rhinoceros of Soul
May 31-June 1, 1968 – Love, The Crazy World of Arthur Brown, Wilson Mower Pursuit, 1st The Psychedelic Stooges
June 7-9, 1968 – Cream, MC5, Carousel, Nickel Plate Express, St. Louis Union, The James Gang, The Thyme
June 14-15, 1968 – The Soft Machine, Wilson Mower Pursuit, Oaesse, The Pack, The Up
June 16, 1968 – "Other Goodies"
June 21-23, 1968 – Blue Cheer, The Jagged Edge, The Soul Remains, The Soul Remains, Nature's Children, MC5, The Psychedelic Stooges
June 28-30, 1968 – Wayne Cochran, Odds Ends, London Fog, Jameson Roberts, Orange Fuzz, The Rationals

July 5-6, 1968 – The Jeff Beck Group, Faith, Charging Rhino of Soul, The Frost

July 11, 1968 – Fleetwood Mac, The Thyme

July 12, 1968 – Pink Floyd, The Thyme, The Jagged Edge

July 13, 1968 – The Who, Pink Floyd, Early Show The Frost, Late Show The Psychedelic Stooges

July 14, 1968 – Toad, Nickel Plate Express, The Third Power

July 19-21, 1968 – Spirit, Fever Tree, The James Gang, The Soul Remains, The Stuart Avery Assemblage

July 26-28, 1968 – The Steve Miller Blues Band, Odds & Ends, Carousel, Air Speed Indicator

August 2-4, 1968 – The Paupers, Rain, Hawk, The Thyme

August 9-11, 1968 – Canned Heat, The Rationals, The Jagged Edge, Children

August 16-18, 1968 – Country Joe & The Fish, Muff, The Pack, H. P. & The Grass Route Movement

August 23-25, 1968 – Albert King, The Rationals, The Jagged Edge, The Psychedelic Stooges, Toad, The Blues Confederation, Dharma, Wilson Mower Pursuit

August 30-31, 1968 – Howlin' Wolf, Chrysalis, The Thyme, Charging Rhinoceros of Soul

September 6-8, 1968 – B. B. King, The Jagged Edge, Wilson Mower Pursuit, The Frost,
The Psychedelic Stooges, Frost

September 13-15, 1968 – Procol Harum, Children, The Third Power, H.P. & The Grass Route Movement, The Thyme

September 20-22, 1968 – The Amboy Dukes, McKenna Mendleson Mainline, MC5, The Up, Rodney Knight, The Psychedelic Stooges

September 27-29, 1968 – Spooky Tooth, The McCoys, Sabbath Opera, Wild Yam Rama Chuck Band, The James Gang

October 4-6, 1968 – Ten Years After, The Rationals, The Dave Workman Band, Orange Fuzz, The Stuart Avery Assemblage, New Phenomena

October 11-13, 1968 – John Mayall, The Frost, The Psychedelic Stooges, Third Power,
The Mind Machine. (Eric Clapton sat in with John Mayall)
October 15, 1968 – Big Brother & The Holding Company, Thyme
October 18-20, 1968 – Kensington Market, Pacific Gas & Electric, MC5, Renaissance Faire
October 25-26, 1968 – Procol Harum, Wilson Mower Pursuit, Carousel
October 27, 1968 – Benefit for Senator Roger Craig.
MC5, The Rationals
October 29, 1968 – Quicksilver Messenger Service, The Frost.
October 30-31, 1968 – MC5, The Psychedelic Stooges.
MC5 Electra Recording Session
November 1-3, 1968 – The Jeff Beck Group, Toad, Mainline, The London Fog, 3rd Joyful Wisdom
November 8-10, 1968 – Buddy Guy, 8th Charging Rhinoceros of Soul, The Lawrence Blues Band, 9th The March Brothers, 10th The Case of E. T. Hooley
November 15-16, 1968 – The Steve Miller Blues Band, The March Brothers, Third Power, The Muzzies
November 17, 1968 – The Moody Blues, The Frost
November 21, 1968 – Blue Cheer, The Stooges
November 22-23, 1968 – Tim Buckley, Terry Reid, Wilson Mower Pursuit, Caste
November 24, 1968 – Jefferson Airplane, The Frost, Terry Reid
November 27-28, 1968 – MC5, The Frost, The Stooges
November 29, 1968 – Blood, Sweat & Tears, Avery Assemblage
November 30, 1968 – The Rationals, Dharma
December 1, 1968 – The Grateful Dead, Popcorn Blizzard
December 6-7, 1968 – Canned Heat, Hamilton Face
December 8, 1968 – Teegarden & Van Winkle, Hamilton Face
December 13-14, 1968 – Deep Purple, Lee Michaels
December 15, 1968 – Benefit for the Salvation Army

Lee Michaels, Frost, Third Power, The James Gang, The Red, White & Blues Band
December 20-21, 1968 – Iron Butterfly
December 22, 1968 – SRC
December 24, 1968 – Arthur Brown, Train
December 26-27, 1968 – Fleetwood Mac, The Rotary Connection, The Stooges, Wicked Religion
December 28, 1968 – The Rationals, The Frost, Caste, Target
December 29, 1968 – Benefit for Senator Roger Craig
Orange Fuzz, Target, Caste
December 30, 1968 – The Fugs, Popcorn Blizzard
December 31, 1968 – SRC, Wilson Mower Pursuit, The Stooges, The Up, The Stuart Avery Assemblage

1969

January 3-4, 1969 – Amboy Dukes, Up, The Pack, Dick Rabbit
January 5, 1969 – The Stooges, Frozen Sun
January 10-12, 1969 – Genesis, Third Power, Caste, James Gang.
January 17-19, 1969 – Led Zeppelin, Linn County, The Lawrence Blues Band, Target, The Wind
January 24-25, 1969 – MC5, The March Brothers, The Train, Piers
January 26, 1969 – Taj Mahal, Asian Flu
January 31, 1969 – Sweetwater, Jethro Tull
February 1, 1969 – Spirit, Jethro Tull, Sweet Wine
February 2, 1969 – Jethro Tull
February 7-9, 1969 – Savoy Brown, Mother Earth
February 14-15, 1969 – Procol Harum, Dharma, Wicked Religion
February 16, 1969 – "Jam Session". Open jam with local bands
February 21-23, 1969 – The Paul Butterfield Blues Band, Van Morrison, The Attack, The Tea, Ball, Sky
February 28-March 1, 1969 – Steppenwolf, Three Dog Night, Mr. Stress Blues Band, The Fruit of the Loom
March 2, 1969 – MC5, Three Dog Night, The James Gang

March 7, 1969 – Procol Harum, Wilson Mower Pursuit
March 8, 1969 – The Jeff Beck Group, Caste, Thomas Blood
March 9, 1969 – Teegarden & Van Winkle, Third Power
March 14-15, 1969 – John Mayall, Savoy Brown, Third Power, Wicked Religion, Phenomena
March 16, 1969 – The Frost, Train
March 21-22, 1969 – Jeff Beck Group, Sweetwater, Dick Rabbit
March 23, 1969 – Sweetwater, Red, White & Blues Band, Sky
March 28-30, 1969 – Sweetwater, The Nice & The Frost, Ebony Tusk, The Flower Company
April 4-6, 1969 – MC5, Pacific Gas & Electric, Wicked Religion, The Maxx, James Gang
April 7-8, 1969 – Jethro Tull, Sky, Caste
April 9-10, 1969 – Savoy Brown, Third Power, Commander Cody & His Swing Band
April 11-13, 1969 – Velvet Underground, The Nice, Earth Opera
April 18-19, 1969 – Chuck Berry, Brian Auger & The Trinity with Julie Driscoll, Rare Earth
April 20, 1969 – "Magical Mystery Tour" screening, Marble Orchard, The Maxx

April 23, 1969 – Benefit for Open City. MC5, The Rationals, The Red, White & Blues Band
April 25-26, 1969 – Canned Heat, Family, The Red, White & Blues Band, Caste
April 27, 1969 – The Stooges, Third Power, All Lonely People
May 1, 1969 – Benefit for the Ann Arbor Argus
May 2 & 3, 1969 – CCR, Churls, The Litter
May 4, 1969 – Taj Mahal, Churls, The Litter
May 9-11, 1969 – The Who, Joe Cocker & The Grease Band
MAY 12, 1969 – The American debut of Tommy! The Who
May 16, 1969 – Led Zeppelin, Sun Ra, Golden Earring. 2 Shows
May 17-18, 1969 – Sun Ra, MC5, Golden Earring
May 21, 1969 – Dr. John, It's A Beautiful Day
May 22, 1969 – The Stooges, It's A Beautiful Day
May 23-24, 1969 – Joe Cocker, The James Gang, Savage Grace
May 30 & 31, 1969 – NO SHOWS - "Detroit Rock & Roll Revival" at the Michigan State Fairgrounds
June 1, 1969 – Private Party for Detroit Rock-n-Roll Revival

June 13, 1969 – Vanilla Fudge
June 14, 1969 – Vanilla Fudge, The Frost, Savage Grace
June 15, 1969 – The Frost, Savage Grace
June 20-22, 1969 – The Bonzo Dog Band, Black Pearl
June 27-28, 1969 – Chuck Berry, Slim Harpo, The Red, White & Blues Band, Sky
July 4, 1969 – CLOSED!
July 5, 1969 – Savoy Brown, Pentangle, Sun
July 6, 1969 – The Grateful Dead, Pentangle
July 18, 1969 – Spooky Tooth, Ten Years After, Stevens Band
July 19, 1969 – Spooky Tooth, Ten Years After, Sand
July 20, 1969 – Spooky Tooth, The Stuart Avery Assemblage
July 23, 1969 – Benefit for the "John Sinclair Defense Fund"
July 25, 1969 – Procol Harum, Man.
July 26, 1969 – The Jeff Beck Group, Sky, Catfish.
July 27, 1969 – Local Bands
August 1, 1969 – Joe Cocker, Sky, Geyda
August 2, 1969 – Joe Cocker, Sky, Chip Stevens Blues Band
August 6-7, 1969 – Frost recording "Rock-n-Roll Music"
August 8, 1969 – Terry Reid, Savoy Brown
August 13, 1969 – Benefit Sen. Craig. The Stooges, Sky, Catfish
August 15-16, 1969 – Bo Diddley
August 20, 1969 – The Frut, The Flow, The Gold Brothers
August 22, 1969 – The Stooges, The Jagged Edge
August 23, 1969 – The Frost, The Stooges, All the Lonely People
August 24, 1969 – Benefit for the Mid-West Printing Co-Op. All the Lonely People, The Up, Sky, Fuchia, Girls Inc.
August 29-30, 1969 – Keef Hartley, Colosseum, The Third Power
September 5-6, 1969 – Johnny Winter, Sky
September 12-13, 1969 – The Turtles, T-Rex, Thomas Blood
September 19-20, 1969 – MC5, Wilson Mower Pursuit
September 26-27, 1969 – The Frost, The Bonzo Dog Band
October 2, 1969 – "Free John Sinclair" Rally
October 3-4, 1969 – Move, Teegarden & Van Winkle, Stooges

October 13, 1969 – Allen Ginsberg, The Stooges
November 7-8, 1969 – The Kinks, Elton John
December 31, 1969 – The Frost, Sky, Richmond, McKenna Mendelson Mainline, Virgin Dawn

1970

January 9, 1970 – Virgin Dawn, Bedlam Riff, Brownsville Station
January 10, 1970 – MC5, Teegarden & Van Winkle, The Red, White & Blues Band, The March Brothers.
January 16, 1970 – Stooges, Wilson Mower Pursuit, The Attack
January 17, 1970 – Golden Earring, Sky, Plain Brown Wrapper
January 23, 1970 – The Wedding of Dave Miller Grande M.C. and Sheila Phillips, Up, Richmond, Woolies, Blues Train, Poison Oak
January 24, 1970 – Sky, Richmond, The Jagged Edge, Shakey Jake, The Up, Floating Circus, The Frut, Virgin Dawn, Blues Train, Shiva. SPEAKERS: Abbie Hoffman, Ken Cockrel
January 25, 1970 – SRC, The Amboy Dukes, The Third Power, Brownsville Station, Frijid Pink, Sun, The Sunday Funnies
January 30, 1970 – NRBQ, Blackwood Drake, Tiers
January 31, 1970 – NRBQ, The Jagged Edge, The Up
February 6, 1970 – SRC, Frijid Pink, The Bhang
February 7, 1970 – All the Lonely People, Plain Brown Wrapper, Toby Wesselfox, The Tribal Simphonia
Feb. 13-14, 1970 – Flamin' Groovies, Shakey Jake, Virgin Dawn
February 20, 1970 – The Frost, Blackwood Drake, Blues Train,
February 21, 1970 – The Frost, Blackwood Drake, Ohio Power, Blackstone Row
October 2, 1970 – John Sinclair Birthday Celebration Party
December 31, 1970 – MC5, The Amboy Dukes, SRC, Cradle, The Jam Band

1971

January 23, 1971 – Benefit for the "Winter Soldier Investigation". Phil Ochs, Justice Colt, Insanity's Horse

January 30, 1971 – Benefit for the 'Ann Arbor Argus'

February 24, 1971 – The Assemblage, The Frut, Holy Ghost, Stonefront, Jam Band

March 17, 1971 – "Benefit for "Youth News Coalition". The Up, John Drake's Shakedown, The Frut, Mutzie, Jam Band

April 8, 1971 – Chuck Berry, The Woolies, Armada, Mutants

April 11, 1971 – SRC, The Third Power, The Frut, Moreefa

April 14 & 15, 1971 – Benefit for MCCC Drop-In Center. The Jagged Edge, Iron Horse Exchange, Proud Flesh, The Jets, The Coming, Joust Limited, Washing Machine

June 6, 1971 – The Flamin' Groovies, The Up, Carnal Kitchen

June 13, 1971 – "Free John Now" Rock-n-Roll Marathon. The Assemblage, The Frut, The Up, Guardian Angel, Brat, Barbara Holliday, Still Eyes

July 29, 1971 – Benefit for the John Sinclair Freedom Fund. MC5, Frijid Pink, The Up, Carnal Kitchen, The Trunion Brothers

August 5, 1971 – Benefit for the John Sinclair Freedom Fund & the People's Ballroom. The Up, The Third Power, Salvage, The Rumor, Pride, Iron Horse Exchange

September 6, 1971 – People's Ballroom Benefit. SRC, The Up, Brat, The Frut, Harvey Khek

September 15, 1971 – Benefit for the John Sinclair Freedom Fund. Commander Cody & His Lost Planet Airmen, The Up, The Motor City Mutants

October 31, 1971 – "Halloween Party & "Grande Re-opening". SRC, The Assemblage, The Third Power, The Frut, The Up, Motor City Mutants, Tacklebox

1972
December 31, 1971-January 1, 1972 – Mylon, MC5, Pacific Gas & Electric, Crabby Appleton
January 24, 1972 – Victory Celebration for John Sinclair. The Up, Harvey Khek, The Motor City Mutants. SPEAKERS: John Sinclair, Mark Stickgold
January 28-29, 1972 – The J. Geils Band, Sweathog, Whiz Kids
February 18 & 19, 1972 – King Crimson
March 21, 1972 – "People's Ballroom Project" meeting
March 25, 1972 – Nova '70 Benefit. The Third Power, The Frut, Harvey Khek, Virgin Dawn, Pegasus, East Side Pair, Bad Manners
March 31, 1972 – Good Friday Tribal Stomp. The Up, The Frut, Harvey Khek, RPM, Iron Horse Exchange
April 1, 1972 – Fool's Party. Jonathan Round, The Werks,
April 13, 1972 – Shadowfax, Thundercloud, Frick
April 23, 1972 – Guardian Angel, Thundercloud
September 30, 1972 – "The Re-Opening of the Grande Party" The Amboy Dukes, MC5, The Motor City Mutants
October 21, 1972 – Catfish, Ted Lucas, The Up
October 22, 1972 – Wishbone Ash, Jonathan Round
October 31, 1972 – Blue Oyster Cult, Capt. Beyond, Wet Nasteez
November 10, 1972 – MC5, The Dogs
November 26, 1972 – Ballin' Jack, Lightnin', Julia
December 31, 1972 – MC5, Roy Buchannan, Jett Black.
(The Last *'Official'* Event.)

**_Did we miss any shows?
Please let us know!_**

FURTHER READING & MEDIA

Motor City Rock and Roll: The 1960's and 1970's
by Bob Harris and John Douglas Peters, 2008

Grit, Noise, & Revolution:
The Birth of Detroit Rock-n-Roll
by David A. Carson, 2005

The Grande Ballroom: Detroit's Rock-n-Roll Palace
by Leo Early. 2016

Louder Than Love: The Grande Ballroom Story - DVD
Produced and Directed by Tony D'Annunzio

Detroit Rock City: Rock-n-Roll in America's Loudest City
by Steve Miller
Audiobook

Detroit Rocks! A Pictorial History of Motor City
Rock-n-Roll 1965 to 1975
by Gary Grimshaw and Leni Sinclair

Devils & Blue Dresses: My Wild Ride as a
Rock-n-Roll Legend
by Mitch Ryder, 2002

The Birth of the Detroit Sound: 1940-1964
by S R Boland and Marilyn Bond

Motor City Underground: Leni Sinclair Photographs 1963-1978

Acid Detroit: A Psychedelic Story of Motor City Music
By Joe Molloy
2002

Please Visit

'Almost' - Da Facebook Page!
https://www.facebook.com/profile.php?id=61551237287631

https://michiganrockandrolllegends.com/

Detroit Rock City on Facebook
https://www.facebook.com/groups/795538003848410

The '60's & early '70's Detroit rock scene:
https://www.facebook.com/groups/56160843006

The Grande Ballroom on Facebook
https://www.facebook.com/groups/tgbdrnrp
https://www.facebook.com/groups/fog1928

SPECIAL THANKS!

A very special thanks to these people without whom this book would not have been possible.

Diane & Chris Bockelman
The Detroit News
Draft 2 Digital
CREEM Magazine
The Bentley Library
Ron Domilici
Mike Olszewski
Ron Bretz
Leni Sinclair
U of M Archives
Helmut Ziewers
Linda Haney
C. Lindow
TL Wescher
Detroit Hour Magazine
Paul Cannon
Ken Barnard
Dale L Roberts
Bruno Ceriotti
Pete 'Grack' Washburn
Ken Barnard
Tom Hawkinson
Jay Fortier
Tom McWhorter
Jerry Basil
Tony Reay

Brittney Bockelman
Sam the Photoshop God
Detroit Free Press
Steve Geer
Don Henderson
Al Jacquez
Editor Courtney Collins
Burton History Collection
Jenifer Veloso
Retro Kimmer
The City of Detroit
Metro Times
Ric Allen Niedzinski
The 5th Estate, Detroit

The Detroit Historical Society

Wayne State University- Public Affairs

The Sharon Harvill Foundation

The Rock-n-Rollers of Michigan!

This book is to honor the forgotten, the overlooked heroes and foot-soldiers of the glory days of Michigan music from 1965 to 1975 a magic decade. It is sadly incomplete and requires much more input from those who were there... those who cheered, those who hitched, those who copped fake ID's, those who made Boone's Farm an institution. It is also for those who humped heavy equipment across parking lots and up stairs in the heat, the cold and the rain...and those who stayed out pass parental curfew! This book will be revised in 2024 with a 2nd Edition... so PLEASE get your recollections and photos in to us to make it REALLY complete. WE THANK YOU!

LONG LIVE MICHIGAN ROCK-N-ROLL!

Tom's Books

- Mr. Mulligan - *The Life of Champion Armless Golfer Tommy McAuliffe*

- NUTS! - *The Life & Times of General Tony McAuliffe*

- Throttle Up - *Teacher Astronaut Christa McAuliffe*

- Mad Dog - *Detroit Tiger Dick McAuliffe*

- Charmed - *From Motown to Combat & Back*

- Almost - *The Road to the Grande*

- Buddy, Brian and Me - *A Spooky Rock-n-Roll Story*

Available everywhere as Books, eBooks and Audiobooks!

Please visit:
www.authortommcauliffe.com

Please send Band info to:
Bookinfo@nextstopparadise.com

Please Leave a Review!

3nd Edition = 2024

Member: Alliance of Independent Authors
Member: Emerald Coast Writers